From the trenches; Louvain to the Aisne, the first record of an eye-witness – Primary Source Edition

Geoffrey Winthrop Young

FROM TRENCHES

FROM THE TRENCHES

LOUVAIN TO THE AISNE, THE FIRST
RECORD OF AN EYE-WITNESS

BY

GEOFFREY WINTHROP YOUNG

LONDON: T. FISHER UNWIN
1 ADELPHI TERRACE W.C.

I wish to express my obligation to the Proprietors of the "Daily News" for permission to use material contributed to their columns.

First Published October, 1914.

CONTENTS

FROM THE TRENCHES

CHAPTER I

The Outbreak. In and Out of Paris.

On Tuesday, 28th of July, I returned from the Alps; the weather conditions had been arctic and the climbing more than usually exciting. During a bathe in the Lake of Geneva, which has become the customary end of the climbing season, I remember saying to my companion, " Well, this is the end of all sensation for the year. Now for the usual dull winter's work."

On Thursday I volunteered to go with the Servian Army as War Correspondent for the *Daily News*, but the European conflagration was already too imminent. On Sunday, it was arranged that I should go to Paris to join the French Army.

FROM THE TRENCHES

The journey started normally. But at New-haven it was startling to see three English travellers turn and rush off the boat at the last minute. It was the first and unforgettable sign of the break-up in our order of life. To take a ticket and start a journey no longer meant the inevitable procession to its end. We were beginning the life of the unexpected; when event and interruption was to take the place of the decent ordering of hours by convention and system.

On the boat were only men; older men called up to the colours. Most of them were fathers of families. One man sat in tears over a photograph of his five children spread out before him. Some had lived all their lives in England. " Well, you're an Englishman, at any rate," said the steward to an obvious cockney. But he was French, though he could scarcely speak it. A very old priest was returning, after twenty years, to " die among his soldier children " in a French frontier village—" or perhaps my grand-children," he corrected, with a faint smile.

As we neared Calais the cloud began to pass.

8

THE OUTBREAK

The men clustered and spoke together: a few started singing. When I had crossed a few days before, the quay had been lined with the usual cheering children, and a few condescending tourists had waved back. Now there was a line of soldiers in the same place. Our passengers rushed to the side and cheered them. A number of French cruisers guarded the entrance. It was the first real proof that we were passing into the facts of war. The odd nightmare feeling of those few first days, that witnessed the collapse of the structure of civilisation upon which our lives had hitherto rested, intensified. The war was true after all; not merely a terrible darkness of sensation into which we kept waking up, with a shrinking discomfort, whenever our attention came back from reading some book or following some ordinary chain of thought.

At Calais there had been no regular train traffic for three days. A number of travellers who had got as far as Calais on previous days decided to return by our boat to England. The porters stood round vaguely, with the distracted strained look that we learned to associate later with the presence of the war atmosphere. I discovered to my surprise a train waiting in the station with steam up :—it was " Lord Kitchener's Special," prepared to carry him on his way to Egypt. But Lord Kitchener at the last moment had not come, for reasons that have since proved amply sufficient. By various persuasive arguments we at last convinced the undecided station-master that as the line had been cleared the express might run through ; and we reached Paris in four hours ; the " last " unofficial express during the war.

The Gare du Nord was empty of porters ; but the long lines of platform were piled ten feet high down the centre with enormous trunks—the abandoned luggage of escaping tourists.

Outside the station the approaches were barred by barriers, where dragoons demanded passes from every foot passenger. Troops poured past, starting for their different centres of concentration. The suburban traffic had ceased. The streets were full of people kept in the town against their will by the demands of the mobilisation.

THE OUTBREAK

Paris had not yet settled down. It was seething in those first three days of panic that seemed throughout Europe to follow the declaration of war. More an atmospheric feeling than a state with definite symptoms. People, for these days, seemed to be moving and speaking semi-consciously, with the nervous suggestion in their faces that they expected something novel and shocking to happen at any second. The supposed German shops and houses were being wrecked and looted. Every now and then there was a hurried rush of feet through the street, as some suspect was hunted or maltreated. The spy-hunting mania seems to have been a universal infection during this time. The disorderly elements in the big towns got the upper hand for the moment and the cold-blooded brutality of these silent man-hunts was to me infinitely more shocking than the sight and sound of the more terrible destruction on the battlefields. It was the first growl of the beast that we had let loose, the savage animal in man waking for our purposes of war. Under my window was a great courtyard, in which hundreds of German

11

and Austrian men, women and children were confined for their protection. They had to sleep on the stones in the open air; and it was a pitiable thing, while the crowds outside the gate were execrating and hustling those who were thrust in to join them, to hear them singing French songs and cheering for France. Most of them were French by education and sympathy, and only German by extraction.

The apache element, which had been encouraged by the thinning out of the Gendarmerie for military service to make patriotism the cover for convenient looting and brutality, was soon brought into order. Cavalry pickets patrolled the streets in the evening; a curious sight, their horses trampling on the pavement of the Rue de la Paix. The worst haunts were raided; many hundreds were arrested, and the police in large motor wagons ran through deserted quarters, stopping and pouncing in batches upon suspected passers-by. The civil hand had released its hold, and it was a day or two before the new military administration could get a firm grip. Government offices were in a not unnatural state of confusion—they had been weakened by the withdrawal of a large proportion of their effective staff, at the same moment that they became responsible for an enormous mass of novel duty. The civilian, under military government, found himself of a sudden unable to move or exist without official permits. The whole social structure had to be reorganised, and the offices were crowded with jostling individuals asking for permissions and explanations which the overworked officials were unable to supply. One of the most painful memories of the war was the sight of refined-looking Austrians and Germans, men and women, artists and writers, with the puzzled hunted expression of people in a nightmare, forced to appeal in public to hurrying footmen and office boys for some indulgence that might allow them to continue to earn their living.

The guiding principle of most public offices at this time, not only in Paris, seemed to be that of sending people backward and forward until their endurance should wear out. With what should happen to them in case they did not comply with all the new regulations the military outlook was not concerned. Every effort was to be concentrated on the preparation for war. The civilian in such an atmosphere has no further rights. If we permit, as nations, the whole civilised order of existence to be pitched into a whirlpool of primitive passions, we must expect to have to scuffle personally for our life-belts.

On the third day of my stay in Paris the situation was indescribably relieved by the declaration of war between England and Germany. The rush on the banks stopped. Prices fell. Money became easier, and the crowd of British and other tourists, sitting on their boxes in nervous lines before the Consulates, diminished. The growing hostility of the Parisians to ourselves disappeared. The organization in the responsible offices, in so far as the public was concerned, began to assume some order.

Night and day the regiments passed through and round the city. The mobilisation was rapid and extremely orderly. There was no apparent hitch. We became confident that the prophecies

that France would be found unprepared
would be proved totally wrong. Gradually
the requisitioned cabs and trams began to
reappear in the streets. The women quietly
stepped into the men's places as ticket-
collectors, etc. With reduced numbers and
closed shops, a graver population took up its
ordinary life.

It was very soon apparent that no official
correspondents were to be allowed with the
French or British forces. A large proportion of
the remaining officials, not to say ourselves,
could have been saved infinite bother if the intention had been declared from the first. After a
week spent without profit in ante-chambers and
bureaus, I decided to get through to Belgium,
where there seemed to be better possibility of
approaching actual events. Chance helped me
to secure a more picturesque fashion of return
than I could have hoped for.

Saturday, August 10th.

I am just back from the first, and " probably
the last," visit that a civilian will be able to pay

15

to the French frontier until the situation has considerably developed.

To have to wait a day in a queue to obtain a permit to leave, another to secure a ticket, and even a third to confirm it by getting a definite seat on a numbered train, can discourage the most patient. The miracle of deliverance, however, took place; and it was brought about by the agency of a chance meeting with a genial chauffeur. There followed an introduction to his employers, a party of Belgian officers returning to their own army, and an amiable invitation to evade some of the weariness of the irregular train journey by taking a lift.

That this was extended beyond all limits contemplated by military regulations must be attributed to a reluctance to turn out on a dark, wet night, in unknown districts, one of a nation whose intervention, as I was assured, has contributed much to the magnificent spirit with which the Belgian troops have supported the first rush of the " invincible machine."

We left Paris with the Boulevards almost

as crowded as ever, but with half the colour and light gone, and a note of unusual gravity in the aspect and talk of the moving stream.

Out through the long, dark suburbs, with the last signal, the flare of the searchlight from the Eiffel Tower, blinking its messages across the clouds high above our heads in front. In the first two miles we were stopped half-a-dozen times; business-like question and answer in quick, suppressed voices. Then the checks decreased as we ran out into the dark fields, though the flash of light upon arms, the challenge and halt came still at bridge and corner. The 'word of the day' passed us at only reduced pace through the larger pickets, but the less well-informed solitary sentry had to be more fully satisfied; and the more, the further from Paris.

Then longer and longer intervals of tremendous racing, unchecked; for the car drove at full speed, and there is no peace traffic! The light of the Eiffel Tower disappeared behind, but there was still the consciousness, in the most remote darkness, that above us darted ceaselessly the continuous stream of wireless messages linking the brain of the army in the little room in unseen Paris with every movement of the vast protecting arms that already lie outstretched to guard France. Through Senlis, Compiègne, St. Quentin, and, at last, Cambrai. It was only possible to calculate the probable towns by the intervals of time, for in each case we were turned off on to side circuits.

When I had passed south to Paris a few days before, on a more westerly line, the country had still seemed inhabited, though by a mixed race: crowds of little red and blue soldiers resting, marching, crammed in troop trains, and knots of men and women at the village corners, or staring at the gates of the huge deserted factories.

Now it seemed an empty land. All the life had passed east into the great war cloud. Only now and again the flash of the lamp on a cluster of boys and older men, sitting or lying by the road; the non-combatants of the villages from the war region tramping west, with blue check bundles tied on the handles of their reaping

18

hooks, to earn what they could, for the later repair of their losses, by helping to harvest. Need for it, too, as the sight of the immense fields of grain, unreaped or half reaped, yellowing the lonely fields of the uninhabited country, suggest ruin to the traveller passing in the train.

Before Cambrai we passed under a thicker darkness of cloud, and met a torrent of rain that for the rest of the night and morning hid everything but the glint of the lamps on falling drops or the more vivid gleam of fixed bayonets.

As we neared the frontier the country seemed to become populous again. The cottages had lights; lights in the fields and through the trees. Only, as we passed, the strangeness increased, for the population had come from a different planet. Quiet cottages, with the glow of uniforms through the wet panes, fields with a few tireless peasant women, helped by good-humoured soldiers, using even the darkness for a desperate effort to get in the forsaken crops. The sight of arms and wagons seemed all the less fitting in the quiet villages because there was no suggestion of war.

FROM THE TRENCHES

One picture stands out vividly; the glare of the lights through the rain on a sentry motionless on guard, while a dozen peasant women, tired doubtless from the day's reaping, slept in his charge, lying under the ridge of the field where they had been working.

Beyond Cambrai I was not at liberty to note our direction or record any details—a natural condition.

In fact, there would be little to record; for the night was a continuance of sounds, of lights, of moving unseen men and horses; and of sudden challenges, coming out of the darkness through the rush of rain. Only I may add that in one village our welcome was marked by a different French intonation as the men gathered round us, and a Belgian advance patrol exchanged jokes with my companions.

Our route from Cambrai, as a matter of fact, took us to Valenciennes, where the Belgian officers left me, hurrying to Maubeuge, while I returned by car to Douai.

In the grey of the morning I emerged, passing north of Douai, and now without my companions.

THE OUTBREAK

As we raced west, still through rain, we passed again into deserted countries. The great machine had done its work. The mobilisation was complete. The dotted sentries, gradually changing from the smart field soldier to the paternal reservist squeezed into a uniform—or partial uniform, seemed the only jetsam of the coloured turmoil of the early week.

The crawling railway, the American ladies complaining of the slow trains and closed buffets, brought us back to ordinary life. Officials, struggling to make us take their passports and their war-regulations seriously, failed to revive any reality of impression.

The war frontier, in rain and darkness, was drifting back into the vague excitement of newspaper reports.

The separation by nationalities was in full progress. France was being cleared of all strangers. The consuls, for reasons not clear, were advising all British residents to return to England at once. The chief sufferers were the children, boys at school in France, children left for visits or cures with French families or in boarding houses. Before I reached Folkestone there must have been at least fifteen such small strays who had had to be adopted and looked after during the succeeding stages of the journey.

CHAPTER II

THE FIRST DAYS IN BRUSSELS

RESTARTING almost immediately, I crossed to Ostend. On the way there were the usual reassuring but unrecordable sights of the sentinel cruisers and busy submarines that made these frequent passages seem, after later weeks in the war countries, like an escape into a comfortable atmosphere of home.

At Ostend a party of efficient St. John Ambulance nurses with whom I had travelled were received with delightful enthusiasm, and free lemonade, by the Belgian soldiers.

Brussels proved a contrast after Paris. The panic days, which took a milder form here in spite of, or because of, the greater proximity of danger, had passed. The townsfolk were absolutely calm, the shops open, the life, except for the absence of means of traffic, undisturbed.

23

FROM THE TRENCHES

Only at intervals, as the chance of the German occupation increased, and the news diminished, there would come over the city for a few hours, one of those electric restless waves which we got to know as signs of approaching danger. They arose from no definite news. The crowds repeated no rumours. It was merely an uneasy feeling in the air. Something had happened far off, and like the unseen fall of a heavy stone in water the ripple reached and spread over the city, that yet had no definite information to disturb it.

Brussels, Monday.

In addition to the well-deserved enthusiasm with which Belgian heroism in arms has been greeted throughout civilised Europe, something must be said of the success with which the extraordinary demands have been met by the departments of the civil administration of Belgium.

During the last few days I have been in contact with a variety of administrative offices in the capitals of three of the belligerent Powers. In one country it seems as yet unrecognised that exceptional conditions demand exceptional organisation. In another there is frank confusion, due to the withdrawal of the majority of the efficient administrative staff to the war and the concentration of the remainder solely on military requirements. Only in Brussels has it been recognised in time that the civil life of a country, properly controlled, is as important to success as any section of the work of mobilisation, and that it is not sufficient to proclaim a state of war and leave everything to an already over-worked military organisation.

Some genius (we know now it was Burgomaster Max) must have been behind the details of city administration here, for in their way they have been as successful in maintaining public confidence as the personality of the mountaineer King has been in inspiring magnificent enthusiasm in his army. The streets are kept orderly, retail trade is almost normal, railway traffic has been rarely interfered with by the immense task of mobilisation; the complications of travellers and passports are simplified and dealt with efficiently and considerately; the Press control is effective but courteous; the hospitals are admirably organised; and the crowds are kept from the stations, on the arrival of wounded or prisoners.

All civil organisations are made use of, and even the Boy Scouts are doing excellent work for all branches, without the error—increasing across the border—of considering themselves semi-combatants. The result is that though the crisis, after the first few days, is being met in all the capitals with gravity and quiet resolution, Brussels—the most immediately threatened—remains a model of civic life under strict but considerate administration.

The moral, if any, is that even in actual war nations are only the weaker for having to send the whole of their manhood to the front. To convert the whole community, with its varied forces of activity, into a single military machine, is to make the machine itself less effective.

Brussels, Tuesday.

I have been given to-day every facility

to inspect the excellent organisation for the care of the wounded. A noticeable feature at the central office is the extent to which amateur help is made use of in organising, and the efficiency and open mind with which unexpected contingencies are met and suggestions considered.

(Later a growing amount of the unqualified " Red Cross " help was found to be open to the same objections that were made to it as the result of our own experience in the Boer War.)

If experience in Paris and Brussels can be turned to account, the British authorities should pay attention to the organisation of private motor-cars lent to the force, to make them of real service. A large proportion are apt to race about without purpose or serviceable return—the usual difficulty with a crowd of enthusiastic would-be helpers.

The prisoners at Bruges confirm the impression that the commissariat arrangements of the advance guard of the invading German columns was very defective, owing to the unexpected resistance. The nature of the wounds

FROM THE TRENCHES

bears out the reports of inexpert German shooting. A great number of the Belgian soldiers brought back from the front are wounded below the knee, and a smaller proportion in the scalp.

The Bruges authorities are most considerate in allowing books and games to be sent to the prisoners of war, and letters to be sent and received. (We were permitted to send down dozens of packs of cards etc., as a distraction for the prisoners.)

The population remains completely calm, even at a time when the next few days may decide their fate. The passage of a German aeroplane yesterday aroused only momentary curiosity. (Every day at about five o'clock the aeroplanes circled over the town. We got to look for them. Almost every night also a bright planet, the " Brussels star " was watched by interested crowds, who took it for a " Zeppelin.")

I witnessed to-day the feeding of some 10,000 children of men at the front. The distribution was excellently organised. Later I saw the distribution of vegetables to the necessitous.

THE FIRST DAYS IN BRUSSELS

These days of anxious waiting are taken with quiet resolution and much good humour.

Brussels, Wednesday.

The gallantry of the Belgian resistance has astonished the world. It has surprised the Belgians themselves. It would be a mistake to look for its source only in the reconstitution of the Army, a matter of the last few years; or to find in it a justification of war, or a plea for national military service as the regenerator of racial vigour.

The war is only the opportunity for the expression of a new Belgian democratic spirit. The new service conditions have been merely one of the agencies by which the idea of the individual right to a greater share in self-government, and the idea of the necessary condition for such government, national independence, have been disseminated.

If the Belgians are fighting heroically, it is because they are fighting for an independence which means not simply a national flag and a coloured space on the map, but individual liberty. They are defending, each man for himself and his neighbour, a responsible share in an increasingly popular Government. The inspiration of the national resistance has been the consciousness in each man of his share of liberty already gained. This democratic spirit has given life and vivid purpose to the military machine.

For the time all difference of party is sunk in securing the primary condition of liberty, racial independence, and the deliverance from the threat of that greatest enemy of freedom and individual enterprise, the military autocracy of Prussia. For the time, that can be the only conscious idea. But the liberal and more intellectual elements must be rejoicing in the realisation that the splendid effect of the new spirit is already justifying the democratic movement by which a share of popular responsibility has been gained in the past. They may well be looking forward to a time when the people will be considered to have earned by their heroism in arms a yet greater part in their own government.

THE FIRST DAYS IN BRUSSELS

The association of M. Vandervelde with the ministry has done much to identify the new spirit of democracy with the central idea of national existence. It is symbolical of the fact that the cause of Belgium is the cause of her people. An ardent advocate of peace and international friendship, he is known to have been one of the most resolutely convinced that, in this crisis of her fate, Belgium could be content with no formal protest, that she must fight for her independence to the last man. (It remains for history to emphasise the measure of political wisdom that the King showed at this crisis, in strengthening the influence of his own resolution, never to allow a free passage to the Germans, by the inclusion in the councils of the nation, of a personality politically antagonistic, but inspired by a patriotism and intellectual power second to none.)

In a country hitherto supposed to have been exceptionally under the influence of clerical domination it is significant to note the very small part that the Church has taken in the time of great emotional strain. In few of the organisations, civil and military, preparatory and corrective, established to meet the crisis, has the Church taken the lead.

Even the Boy Scouts, as a small instance, who loom large in the administrative life of Brussels for the time being, and who have hitherto been divided into hostile camps by Church and lay divisions, have sunk their differences, and are absorbed into the non-sectarian and civil machinery. It will be interesting to see what effect the loss of grip of the Church at this crucial moment may have upon her position when the new Belgian national spirit, confirmed by trial, can turn its energies again to problems of government and personal liberty.

The renaissance, or rather reassertion, is not confined to men. Women are taking a prominent part, and that not only in replacing men in subordinate work. It has not been elsewhere stated, but I have been assured by several of the wounded that much of the power of resistance in the Liége forts is due to the women of the town of Liége, who twice a day risk their lives in visiting the forts, bringing provisions and new heart.

With such wives and mothers there is little reason to fear that the new spirit will be limited to one generation, or can be accounted for as merely the reaction from a war fever. The war will but harden it into manhood.

CHAPTER III

The Belgian Engagements : Eghezee, Haelen

In a country, or town, under war conditions, all the usual facilities of civilisation are suspended. Post, telegraph and train cease, so far as civilians are concerned. Trams, carriages and automobiles are required for military purposes. Movement out of, or even within, a town is practically stopped. Not only are the countries sorted out by nationalities, but even each town and village. A strange face is an object of suspicious inquiry. A stranger finds it difficult to stay at places where he is ; it is all but impossible for him to leave them. Permits of a particular kind are needed for any journey ; and these are constantly changing. The precautions are, of course, necessary, especially to counteract an elaborate spy-system, such as that of the Germans. They place, however, immense diffi-

34

culties in the way of war correspondence. To get the necessary permits for motor travel, the only method of safe passage for a correspondent, is a matter of much time and difficulty. When they are obtained, there remains to find a car still unrequisitioned, and the services of a driver free from military service and of absolutely sound nerves. In this I was exceptionally fortunate. To "Lèon the chauffeur" is due the success which attended my first efforts to get near the battle line, our pleasant reception in almost all cases there, and our not infrequent escapes from awkward situations. I was able to make some small return in the rescue of his jolly family of babies from Brussels on the morning of the German entry.

Our first excursion towards the actual fighting was a race down the Belgian lines as far as Namur, to visit the French troops. They had then just reached the Meuse, and were lined, holding the bank towards Dinant.

Liége had fallen. A few forts were said to be holding out; but communications were cut off.

FROM THE TRENCHES

A dash down the fighting lines to the south to-day showed us at points along the route signs of the fierce little fights which have taken place. The Belgians have held their positions magnificently.

Our car was stopped every few miles to convey wounded. In these hot days the troops, lying waiting along the trenches, have been greatly suffering from the sun. The Belgian army cap is highly unpractical. We carried a load of some five thousand handkerchiefs, which were distributed, as well as the usual journals and cigarettes.

There were intervals of sunlit fields—then masses of dark uniformed troops. Occasionally chains and wire entanglements appeared suddenly through the trees by the wayside.

French troops—jolly fellows, fit and in great spirits—were in Namur. The sight of cyclists returning from the little victory at Eghezee, garlanded with flowers, was tremendously acclaimed.

As we returned in the exquisite summer night

36

we kept passing the shadows of moving troops in the thin darkness. Three times we heard the sound of sabots and singing, where the peasants and children were gathered round the priests, under the trees, in supplicatory services to the Virgin. As a contrast, twice again during the rush home through the night there was a flash and report from a nervous sentry, and one bullet struck our car.

The Belgian army lay along the line Diest, Tirlemont, Jodoigne, stretching towards Namur. The Headquarters were at Louvain. It covered Brussels, and at the same time anticipated a flanking movement on the north, by Hasselt. The main body occupied field trenches and forts protected by wire entanglements. It was continually harried by the countless bodies of roving Uhlans, and suffered considerably from the heat, as it lay unoccupied in the trenches. It had done magnificently in the forts; how would it do in the field? It was a time of waiting, of small distracting engagements. None of us knew where the real stroke would fall.

I spent the next few days at Louvain and in

various villages on the lines, visiting the wounded in the cottages and shelters.

Thursday.

Barricades and guards on every road. The country absolutely at peace. The peasants working at the crops. But " the Prussians "—for we do not speak of " Germans "—are pressing us on the north ; they are threatening and breaking in on the south. The first menaces, but the second may compel our retreat on Antwerp.

As we run out of Brussels down the shady avenues we are blocked by little mazes of tram-cars, dragged across the road. Further on, at every corner, crossing and hamlet, there are barriers of waggons, of driven logs or piled trees. From these the Civil Guard threaten with levelled guns. Dangerous citizens, in mediæval hats ; they loose off on suspicion, and are as zealous as most amateurs. They will run on to a roof to shoot at an aeroplane 2,000 feet above them, regardless of damage that may be done by their falling bullets.

Further from the town the uniforms get more patchy ; a bowler hat with the colours of Belgium round it is one of the smartest insignia. In the hamlets we have the peasants in blouses; but with business-like rifles, readily handled. Good fellows; stern on their job; but, once satisfied, ready to laugh back and exchange news. And everywhere ubiquitous jolly children, scrambling about, even on the barriers behind the bayonets. A little blue monster, with a large bottle, hopped and chuckled with glee as a surly guard all but fired on us from mere boredom.

We are racing down the line to Namur. Small engagements with Uhlans are of hourly occurrence to-day in the domestic-looking fields. The chateaux are deserted. Everyone has an anxious eye on the horizon.

My red ensign is saluted cheerily by the soldiers, but it has to be explained to the sturdy peasant guards. An officer stops me to tell me that I am an Englishman, and to explain that he is riding on a horse this morning captured from the Germans. The German horses are good; but the Belgians ride better.

We are practically among the Namur defences. The challenges come every two minutes, or less.

FROM THE TRENCHES

The fields are scarred with modern "forts"; great wire entanglements, twisted boughs, and red and yellow trenches, sometimes roofed with the new-cut crops. Little bodies of soldiers, small, wiry, intelligent men and boys, with pleasant faces already rough with exposure, crowd round to chat and to welcome the cigarettes and newspapers.

"There has been a skirmish here," they tell us; "Two prisoners are in that cottage"; "Three wounded in the church"; and again and again they ask, "Where are the English?" and "How many are the French?" Ah, if we knew! For the Belgian army has played the hero in fort and open field; but many know they are hard-pressed. Our talk is of the demoralisation of the Germans, and of their hunger when captured.

In the middle of a little green wood, sheltered from aeroplanes, suddenly we are in a fort. Vicious guns are trained on to a cottage-hedge in full flower, that has been left standing to screen them for the time. Close beside them, some twenty boys are bathing in a shady pool. But they are curiously quiet. The chances of

40

fight and death are too near. And, as in all wars, there are terrible stories growing of the savagery of the enemy.

Dark, waspish little soldiers lie seemingly at haphazard through the fields, and they fill the streets of Namur. The town is oddly still. Even the huge masonry of the fortress, hanging above the beautiful wooded gorge of the Meuse, seems to share in a suppressed, shifting quiet of expectancy.

We wheel out of the town, this time not to see again our French friends, but away to where the pressure is closest. Only last night an audacious German detachment of some 300 pressed within a few miles of the town, at Eghezee, and paid for its folly. Taking possession of the Chateau of Boneff, they looted the house, and sat down to cook rice on the stubble slope by the road. An airman marked them down. A small body of Belgians crept along the road, from Namur, " on all fours," occupied the trenches already prepared in the potato slope opposite —finding no sentries or outposts—and swept the detachment at close range. Prisoners, dead, and wounded, few were able to retreat; but the remainder had some revenge a few hours later on a rash cyclist contingent of Belgians which followed them too far.

While I walked the field the horses were still being charred and buried, the saddlery and cooking pots collected.

Cavalry patrols of dark, hard-bitten little soldiers speckled the country round. A careworn young lieutenant arrested me the first time. He hardly attended to the papers, rolling a cigarette and murmuring courteously and constantly: "There are so many spies about."

As we pushed on and out on field tracks for a further view, the car appeared to materialise a succession of cantering patrols out of the empty sunlit spaces of fields. Some were courteous: some not. But all, fortunately, had more serious business to attend to in the end.

At last we spied a more stealthy line of jogging helmets circuiting behind trees far ahead. This time we decided that arrest, even after a race, would be the lesser risk to take. We turned and spurted back, our doubts confirmed by seeing two or three unexpected lines of dots concentrating upon us or our pursuers. We spun through them and back on to the larger road. A few shots heard later, a long way behind, gave us the feeling of having acted as a convenient decoy for at least one party of the dreaded Uhlans.

Our next arrest, shortly afterwards, was by a fierce-looking commandant, on an exceptionally fine horse. He was softened by the red ensign and the success of his own attempts to talk English. We agreed that it was difficult to make certain when we were or were not well within the front, since the two forces were " all in and out along here." He, too, wished to know " Where are the English ? " He had captured two dragoons that day with his own hand. Some of his troops had the metal German lances slung on their shoulders.

On our straight run back to Namur, by entanglements and trenches and constant challenges, we watched with pleasure an aeroplane circling above the tremendous hill fortress; certainly, we thought, a Belgian, because of its low flight.

FROM THE TRENCHES

Half-an-hour later, as I was getting food in the lively centre of the town, there came the now familiar rush of the highly-strung crowd. In a small cart, supported by four workmen, an old, respectably-dressed shopkeeper was being drawn to the hospital with shattered legs and terribly wounded head. He had been struck down in the street by the explosion of a dynamite hand-grenade, flung from the aeroplane which we had watched circling against the sunset. The senseless, wanton savagery of war.

Our return in the dark seemed likely to be sensational, for rumour had it that the Prussians were pressing in again on the north near Wavre. Up to Wavre we merely had the not infrequent incident of a guard, who had forgotten to light his lamp to stop us, trying to repair his omission by firing after our tail-lamp.

At Wavre, in the half-lit street, we met stretchers passing through the mute groups of men and children, a grim sign of near conflict.

Here a genial commandant stopped me for a talk. He had been at Eghezee, and was now

on his way to " receive " a small German column
that was pushing in on the east under cover
of night. A surprise had been arranged by the
Belgians.

He brought me up the road north-east from
Wavre. We left the car under dark trees; and
he directed me to a hillock on the right. After
an age of waiting, little dispersed flashes and
reports came from the hollow in the dark in
front. The Germans were getting into touch.
It was the first time I had heard the mitrailleuse,
like the ripping of rough canvas.

Answering flash and snarl came from a rough
semicircle of shadow in front and on the south
side of them. Larger guns came into action
on the north, muffled behind slopes. There is
little to see by day in a modern battle unless one
takes part. Nothing to see at night. I was due
back. When I left the commandant, to return
through Wavre, the stretchers were passing
through empty streets.

It was not yet apparent what line the German
northern armies were about to adopt for their
main advance. The Uhlan screen prevented

45

exact reconnoitring. We were aware that ⸜ French troops were coming up ; and there seemed to be signs that they intended either to throw across a number of regiments to assist the Belgians east and south of Brussels, or to form a continuous line with the Belgian army on a curve from Diest to Namur. The latter plan would have forced a great battle in the neighbourhood of Genappe, south of Waterloo. At the same time I was aware that the Government were anxious both on account of the small numbers of French crossing the frontier and at the apparent slowness of their advance. We did not know of the strategy that had concentrated the French armies upon Alsace-Lorraine, or, consequently, of the time necessary for the alteration of the balance of troops towards the north. It was rumoured, as it appears now among the Germans also, that the British force would either advance by Brussels, and hold a position in the centre of the defensive loop from the north of Hasselt to the French positions upon the Meuse and Sambre, or cover Antwerp and the Belgian left wing, thus preventing a turning movement of the Germans along the frontier of Dutch Limburg.

The position became clearer when the news arrived of the advance of German army corps across the Meuse; and of the great concentration that was proceeding in the neighbourhood of Hasselt. It was still supposed, however, to be largely a movement of cavalry.

Heavy fighting was reported on Thursday and Friday at Haelen. Friday was a brilliant sunny day. It was full of surprises. We forced our way along rough lanes, to run suddenly into small reserves or batteries hidden from the aviators under trees. At times we had to move hazardously with one wheel in a ditch, as we passed lines of munition waggons, or crowded along jogging lines of cavalry. We skirted behind the trenches from Louvain to Diest, and thence to Haelen.

Haelen, Friday.

Fine fellows these little Belgians; intelligent and quick to respond. Rather weary now and strained, for many of them have been already long in the field. Day and night they have been fighting at odds of ten to one. They are men who think, and they fight the better for it. A desperately exhausting fight it is. Dispersed in parties over their immense front, they have to rush and concentrate the moment that one of the small squadrons of German cavalry, infinitely scattered, is signalled. Some, thus, have been in three separate engagements on one day, in different places. But they are as stout-hearted as ever. Tell them what the world thinks of their heroism, and they smile with half humorous pleasure. Tell them what we guess of the nearness of their allies, and they crowd round with an unselfconscious delight that is not for themselves but for their nation and their cause.

As we pass among them, in their " rest " moments, it is easy to make them cluster, laughing like a crowd of alert boys ; but in the fighting line they are tense as wires, with a concentrated sternness that the Germans are learning to respect.

" I have sabred two this morning," a powerful, brown-faced lad, a cavalryman, who had just finished bandaging a German dragoon with a broken back, said to me drowsily to-day. This was in a cottage at Haelen.

Haelen, the wrecked village, where the Belgians have proved their heroism in the field, has to-day been the scene of renewed attacks and unshaken resistance. The Germans, who lost 2,000 out of 5,000 in the two days' fighting, had to fall back upon the base of their army corps at Kermpt; but they have been pressing, pressing forward again in overwhelming numbers.

The fields outside the village are a terrible sight: littered with dead men and horses, broken guns, twisted lances. In one trench alone twelve hundred Germans were being buried, and the harrow was passed over the brown scar as soon as it was filled in. Cottages burned and black with shell fire, with dead cattle in the sheds. There were furrows where the shell had ploughed; and trampled heaps in the crops and among the bloodstained roots, where the charging horses had been mown down in masses.

Among the fragments of leather and helmets were a number of scraps of letters and postcards, carried by the soldiers in case of death, and a German collection of sacred songs for the campaign. These things are better left as they lie, and it is unwise, in running between rival armies. to risk carrying " mementoes " of battle. One very touching letter, however, that I found here, was carried home by a friend, and as my translation has already appeared, it may be reproduced :

" Sweetheart,

Fate in this present war has treated us more cruelly than many others. If I have not lived to create for you the happiness of which both our hearts dreamed, remember that my sole wish is now that you should be comforted. Forget me. Create for yourself some contented home that may restore to you some of the greater pleasures of life.

For myself, I shall have died happy in the thought of your love. My last thought has been for you and for those I leave at home. Accept this, the last kiss, from him who loved you."

THE BELGIAN ENGAGEMENTS

A German biplane hovered overhead as I examined the positions in the field. I was anxious to make sure of the German line of advance. I drove forward over the village bridge, the scene of savage fighting and bombardment, but still just standing, and unexpectedly found myself behind the fighting line, facing a renewed German advance. Every house in the village was wrecked and looted. The street was littered with broken bottles and remnants. The church tower was gaping with holes : the Belgians, too, had had to use it to train their guns upon, during the German occupation. The walls still standing were pierced for rifle fire.

As we moved across the long-contested bridge and up the broken bullet-scarred street it was to the sound of cannon. Waggons bringing up fresh ammunition poured past us. On the stones under the walls knots of soldiers, too weary to shift their feet, lay sleeping during their hour of release from the front.

At intervals round the battered church wall came the stretchers, with the still more quiet dead.

FROM THE TRENCHES

I had visited three field ambulances along the line from Louvain during the day. Now for the fourth time I was admitted to the improvised ambulance rooms, well knowing what I should find. For the Belgian remains true to his civilisation. The wounded German prisoners, as they came in, were treated with just the same care, their death dignified with the same respect as that of our own friends. And yet the stories that are told of their cruelty to the peasants, and sincerely believed by the soldiers, are terrible. " But "—said a little rough, unshaven peasant infantryman to me—" we are men who feel. Whatever our enemies may do, we shall continue as we have begun—to the end."

I was even allowed to speak to some of the wounded in their own language. Not one had a word of complaint. Poor fellows, they all believed they had been fighting against the French! I think two of the finest men I have ever seen were a Belgian corporal and a German private, who lay dying to-day of bullet wounds, in half-burnt villages a few miles apart. In the cottage yard a peasant woman, with four children round her, who had seen her house sacked, was making coffee over a wood fire for the wounded Germans.

But the air round us was overcharged. The Belgians had been surprised in some woods as they advanced from the village this morning. They had lost heavily. Now they were holding the position well, but the Germans, in spite of losses, were closing in. Their advanced firing parties were at the moment within 300 yards of the village. At any instant their cavalry, whose lances and helmets lay mixed with smashed bottles about the village square, relics of the past day, might sweep round the defence.

All of a sudden one of the changes of mood common to nerves at such crises came over the soldiers about us. The faces hardened. We were under arrest. The fact of my talking German to the wounded, a mistake I learned to avoid later, was sufficient to brand me a spy. I had taken the precaution to translate each sentence to the sergeant in charge, but he denied it when I referred to him. Men in the " war state " are hardly responsible. I was taken, by the sentries, past a barricade, held by infantry with Maxims, to the headquarters. The major commanding, furiously issuing orders, sending out supports, etc., from the parlour of the last cottage in the street, was too occupied to give me full attention. " I have the right to shoot you : you ought to be shot, of course," was all he had time to exclaim at intervals. After a hurried, unsatisfactory talk I moved outside, and waited, among sullen faces. And I could see, a few yards off, the little sunlit glade of trees, where the Belgians were moving and firing, as they covered the entrance to the village.

An important prisoner was hurried in, and then away in a car. In the bustle some change occurred. Another major was in command. A tall, scholarly-looking man, utterly incongruous in such a scene, shouting abrupt orders in a cultivated voice. At last he had a moment for me. " I am perfectly satisfied ; but we are in war. You will, I hope, excuse my forbidding your advance ; in fact, it is impossible : the enemy command the road : good day "—he bowed me out with my guard. Immediately only sunny faces round us again ; but still with the fixed, absent eyes, that tell of danger, close and realised.

It had not been my wish to advance further. In fact, the car was already turned, ready for a race back if the Germans broke in. We waited for a few more minutes to laugh that look out of the eyes of our friendly soldiers. Then we moved slowly back along the line of ruins, the traces of death, that made but a single battle-field of the fight of to-day and the fights of two days ago. We zigzagged through the sleeping soldiers, stretched unstirring on the cobble stones. The roar of a German aeroplane passed again over our heads ; and the firing sounded nearer, both to north and south.

As I circled towards Diest, the roads were choked with munition and reinforcements. A column of infantry wheeled to take up a position in a beet-field on our left. A squadron of cavalry in the brown busby clattered past to head off Uhlans reported on our right. The village streets were barricaded with waggons ; but the crowds of anxious, waiting women, boys, and children laughed and chaffed back at us as we waited at the barriers on the roads for a gap to be made for our passage.

Supports, and more waggons, and the constant rushing cars of officers. The orchards were full of cavalry horses, many of them captured from the Germans. The waiting soldiers grinned as I remarked on the fact that some of them were wearing the boots of German prisoners, even German regimental breeches. The Belgian mobilisation had to be carried out in two days. Many of the troopers have had to complete their kit at the German expense.

An officer swung into the car. He had come out of Liége to "rest." He is one of the only two survivors of the party of seven who fought hand to hand with and killed the seven or more Germans who rode into Liége to assassinate General Léman. "We watched them riding up the street; they were waving a white flag. My friend said, 'They have just killed a sentry.' We fired—thus; and they fired; and their four officers fell; and the others we killed; but only two of us were left."

THE BELGIAN ENGAGEMENTS

As the sun set, long processions of Red Cross waggons, followed by lines of trudging assistants, and some priests, blocked the roads.

The troops were moving back into cantonments. A Division was being sent back to " rest." They swarmed over the fields and surged round the car for news. Through the wire entanglements, and over the trenches and bough-fortifications pressed a host of women. A number of wives and mothers, who had come long distances for a last sight—some of them had walked over twenty miles to find the right quarter—were thrust at us enthusiastically from the roadside, and the car was filled so as to save, if only a few of them, the twelve miles of tramp to a railway. Many had carried heavy baskets of provisions; but the troops are so well fed that they were not needed. Delicate, educated women, they waved courageous farewell to their husbands, private soldiers with serious sensitive faces, men of the learned professions, and poured into my ears the stories of hardship that their men were undergoing.

As we passed, the towns seemed full of silent

57

women waiting for news. Small bodies of troops moved out now and again across the market squares to repulse approaching Uhlans.

At one town we traversed, Louvain, the King was in council with the staff. At Diest a huge crowd was acclaiming a joyful report about the English, that sent us, too, on our way with very particular reason for cheering.

In the last run in, through the dark, we were again made useful : this time to convey a special mission to the War Office in Brussels.

The Germans entered Diest soon after we left.

This was the beginning of the great German flood, that lapped like a slow tide from Hasselt, to Haelen, to Diest, and bursting upon Louvain in the next days, poured irresistibly across Belgium.

CHAPTER IV

Namur and the French Lines

THE news of the evening was that of the battle at Dinant: the great drawn battle that distracted attention from the launching of the bolt of the main German advance from Hasselt, north of the Meuse. Even the layman could see the result must delay the French design—if it was their design—of joining up with the Belgians to cover Brussels. It was vital, if Belgium was not to be abandoned, that the French should get up in time. Early the next morning I forced a way once again to Namur, with the hope of possibly reaching Dinant, and, if not, of finding out the real strength of the French in the region round Namur. One road was still open.

Namur was under the cloud of that silent nameless panic that is more terrible than tumult.

FROM THE TRENCHES

It is not found in the fighting lines; only in the threatened civilian towns occupied by military headquarters in face of the enemy. Nerves strained to snapping point find their only vent in black suspicion. As a stranger, to catch a passing eye is to challenge insult or arrest. For two days I was the only unofficial visitor in the town. I was arrested five times. I could not sit for five minutes at my window without hearing the tramp of civic guards or police on the stairs, coming to interrogate me. My room was searched twice a day for wireless apparatus. On the second occasion I pointed out, sarcastically, that the small drawer of the wash-hand stand had not been searched. It was never left unexamined again! There was no definite news of advance, but absence of news is the worst trial to civic nerves. Fear was in the air. But it was restrained and silent. A lifted voice in the street was followed by a little noiseless rush of people. On the second day I did not venture a hundred yards from the hotel, to avoid the wearisome arrests and interrogatories.

NAMUR AND FRENCH LINES

Namur, Saturday.

Under my window the crowds are waiting round the station for news. The trains are practically stopped; there may be one to Brussels to-morrow. Only one road to the north is open; the others are closed, completing the circle of fortification. Yesterday the aviators were dropping bombs on to the line opposite. To-day the town is quiet, but humming restlessly. The thunderstorms may have checked the pestilent persecution, or possibly the Germans now know all they need.

South of us, on the Meuse, the two northern armies, French and German, are facing one another. They were in conflict all yesterday, and there is no reason now to keep silence about the positions. The scouting Uhlans, whom I touched at Eghezee and east of Wavre, have done their work. The main body of the German Army Corps, supposed here to be the 4th, possibly with the 10th in support, appears to be moving definitely against the French to the south of the fortress. . . .

All day yesterday, in a sanguinary battle,

61

they were trying to force the passage of the Meuse north and south of Dinant. A squadron of French Dragoons was surprised beyond the river and destroyed. There are the wildest reports as to the losses of the Germans. An eye-witness of the attempts upon the Anseremme Bridge described to me the Germans as swept by the guns, as they advanced in their usual columns, and unable to fall as they died, so close and massed were the ranks.

They were repulsed at the time, but they are returning in force. They have began an attack upon the fort across the river at Davre. The armies seem to be advancing north-west into the great angle of the Meuse at Namur, coming into touch with the Belgians and French along the semi-circle from Huy to Givet.

In a lonely little village south of Namur to-day, where I shared the deserted street with a few sad-faced women and half a dozen cripples and old men, the landlord said, " This is the 15th : our feast day. I usually have hundreds of tourists ; to-day you are alone ; we are waiting for the great battle. To-night ?—

to-morrow ? Who knows ? " As he spoke, and we waited, the thunderstorms kept rolling up the lime-stone gorges, and we listened, each time thinking this was the beginning.

I slipped down from Namur this morning along the front of the French lines on the Meuse. In all the villages deserted houses ; walls pierced for musketry ; wire entanglements ; and the picturesque windings of the river scarred with trenches, and stirring with hardly-seen troops. It was a curious change to leave our little friends, the dark Belgians, and meet the moving patrols of French Dragoons, large, splendid-looking fellows, bronzed and hardened since I saw them leave Paris but a fortnight ago. But they cannot show more heart than our worn little Belgian comrades, as they held back the overwhelming numbers in those desperate engagements I watched yesterday, at Haelen and Diest.

Where the cliffs on the far side sink to the river the roadside hedges on this bank were lined with smart, keen-looking infantrymen, by hedge and tree and trench, leaning across walls or behind trees, with rifle ready. Hardly an eye turned on us. For on the hills across and to the south the Germans have been sighted. The attack may come anywhere, any time.

We got within a mile of Dinant, well within the entrenched lines; past barriers and fortified bridge ends—where the soldiers lay ready under screens of sheaves. They were naturally suspicious at first of civilian dress, but always courteous. Journals delighted them. One smart dragoon, being shaved under a bough-shelter, musket on knee, received his first wound in jumping up to ask for a newspaper, and to cheer for England.

At last came the final block. "Impossible to proceed; no despatch-carrier even may pass." Infantry were clustered about us, keenly watching the other bank. The shimmer of the light blue cavalry uniform stirred and glittered up the steep lane behind us, hidden and ready to charge and sweep the bridge clear.

As the car raced back along the lines, even those who had chatted on our first passing, or turned to salute, had barely a glance for us. Something was in the air. The most talkative

of the captains who had questioned us looked
at our passing with only the absent inward
look familiar now on the faces of men going
into action. The dragoons moved restlessly
along the road in quick patrols, carrying news
of the enemy sighted in the woods on the opposite
bank. The road is exposed in all its length, and
the car was so conspicuous that I expected
every instant to be fired upon from the trees
opposite. A long train of guns wound out of
Namur and blocked our entry.

What they awaited may come to-night, or
to-morrow. We should hear the guns here if
the siege had begun in earnest.

Later.

A bomb has just exploded on the line opposite my window. The glass roof of the station
is shattered.

The sound of guns has begun from the forts
on the east.

Namur, Sunday midnight.

The French were engaged last night at Dinant,
even before we were clear of their lines. An

attempt of the Germans to cross the Meuse at Bouvignes was repulsed with loss.

The Belgians this afternoon repulsed an attack at Wierde, east of Davre, the fort on the defences of Namur across the Meuse, where an unsuccessful attempt was made yesterday.

I was out on the lines of the defences to-night with some friendly soldiers, sharing their supper. I may say the commissariat of the Belgians is excellently managed. The soup was first-class, and some of the wives, just back from a Sunday visit to their husbands, tell me their extra burden of food and wine was not needed by the men. One woman, white with dust, had walked thirty miles in search of her son to-day. In the end an officer was found to send her forward in a Red Cross car.

Even as I supped in the dark on the outworks with those soldiers, one of the strange mood changes that are getting familiar in the war atmosphere took place. Sullen suspicious looks, whispered questions round me. I withdrew quietly but quickly. (When we hear the true story of the fall of Namur, this too may have to be taken into account. Soldiers conscious of their terrible losses, a populace half-believing itself deserted by its allies. French troops sent in, and again hurriedly withdrawn. The Namur army cut off from its main body, from the king, and the command.)

This evening the 28th Belgian Regiment marched in in triumph from its successful engagement yesterday at Lothain.

Only the First, Second and Third Division have yet been engaged. They have borne alone the whole weight of the recent fierce engagements in the front, from Namur to Diest. To-day the Third, here, is being replaced by the Fourth.

The Fifth and Sixth are still in reserve. They will probably be kept to cover Antwerp, if Brussels falls. The Sixth is the élite of the Army. The Belgian shooting so far has corrected the inequality of numbers; but the Sixth Corps contains the chosen marksmen. The Germans continue to shoot low.

The trains this evening stopped running for the reason that a column of 150 German cavalry has been located across the line and along the road down which we ran this morning; and the Belgians have been preparing a surprise for to-night. In fact, there is an additional, more serious and most satisfactory cause, almost laughable in its performance to anyone in the secret, of which again I may not at present speak. (French troops were being run in concealed by various devices from the sight of the airmen. They detrained outside the town. A regiment of "Turcos" however marched in in the evening, and produced the first applause I had heard for a long time).

The aviators have stopped dropping bombs. The soldiers, at least, believe to-night that "the King has sent an envoy to say that a hundred prisoners will be shot for every bomb dropped in the unprotected streets." Only girls and old men have so far suffered from the inhuman practice.

I have spoken with two witnesses of the encounter about Dinant yesterday. The chief struggle raged round the ancient citadel which was taken and retaken. The French guns smashed the pontoon bridges as soon as the

Germans had built them. The permanent bridges were swept as the columns advanced. They were mined, but left standing, acting each as a death trap. The impatience of the French African troops, the "Turcos," who are spoken of with bated breath, is said to have prevented the success of a crushing enveloping movement, a yielding in the centre to pour in on the flanks, which the French could only partially execute.

Pitiable stories are told of the *corps-à-corps* charges of the "Turcos." The stories are becoming so universal that there seems reason to suppose that the German "machine" has not been trained to meet the bayonet. The Belgians have already learned to count on the bayonet as their strongest weapon in meeting the Uhlans.

The battles at Haelen would suggest that the tubular Uhlan lance is less serviceable than the Belgian bamboo. It is certainly ineffective against the solid bayonet. At Haelen I found a large number of "buckled" and cracked lances along the line of the German cavalry charges.

FROM THE TRENCHES

The losses yesterday about Dinant seem to have been immense. Rumour speaks of anything between 20,000 and 40,000 put *hors de combat* from the two opposing forces. It is probable from accounts that the number must be reckoned in thousands. A peasant from a village below Dinant told me that when he was called back from the fields "by the noise" he "came over the hill to see the Meuse running red-streaked with blood."

Allowing for the Ardennois emotion, there seems no doubt that the fighting was savage and terribly costly, and that one of the many good reasons that stopped our passage just short of Dinant was the fact that the dead were not yet removed.

In this war both sides are very rightly concealing their losses. The relatives are separately informed, whenever it seems fit; and no lists are published.

To-night it is reported among the soldiers, and possibly therefore with truth, that the Belgians have just blown up and abandoned one of the smaller forts. "The reinforcements came just a day too late; the 4th Army Corps should have been up yesterday."

The German corps lately engaged at Haelen and Diest in the north are reported to be moving south-west from their base at Kermpt and Hasselt. If this is true, the movement indicates a general advance preparatory for the battle of the three (four?) armies.

We know the next move, so far as one side can know it, but it must be left to explain itself. A few days, and the board in this corner will have been disclosed.

Monday, 7 a.m.

The surprise joke for the Germans, referred to above, has been going on all night.

Regiments of the 4th Belgian Army Corps have also been detraining all morning. Fresh, brisk-looking men, curiously pallid compared with their black unshaven comrades, who have been in the field all the week. Better booted and equipped, having had more time to mobilise. Odd boots and German prisoners' breeches, belts, and trappings have become common sights in that hard-worn division. A little captain at

71

FROM THE TRENCHES

Diest was wearing blue breeches, one brown riding boot, one regulation black, a kepi with two bullet-holes through it, and a green Chasseur coat too small for him. " What would you ? I have been in five fights, from Liége to Diest ; the Germans sacked my lodging on the night at Haelen. I fought them there without a coat. We were seventeen in the corner of the wheat, cyclists ; at night I went back with the two other survivors, and found my bicycle. One is a philosopher ! one must be gay ! "

The Second, Third, and Fourth Regiments of the Line have suffered most. The Second have lost a large proportion of their numbers.

The proportion of officers killed is very large ; this especially among the Germans, owing to their massed formations and the distinction in uniform.

I saw a letter last night, found on a German officer, bitterly complaining of the want of preparation, absence of proper scouting. and reckless waste of life in their mass attacks.

Little credence can be attached to stories of an enemy's savagery. But a circumstantial story has been twice told me by men in different companies that Belgian prisoners were placed in the front line in the engagement at Landen; and that the Belgians fired low at first until their friends had fallen, shot in the legs. I give it only for what it is worth.

There is no doubt that the battle in which the Belgians lost most heavily was an early engagement on the Tirlemont lines, where, in the dark, two regiments of Belgians mistook their line, and fired on each other. Both lost many men. Under present conditions this must occur. The airmen are asking that no aeroplane shall be fired upon. They suffer from their friends.

Namur, Monday night.

Have you seen a fight between a hawk and a rook, or a hawk and peregrine? That, or something like it, took place over the open square by the station this afternoon.

An aeroplane appeared out of the west; it soared over the railway against the cloudy sky, stooped, and suddenly, as if struck, shot with a steep volplane on to this side of the Meuse.

FROM THE TRENCHES

There was a rush of cars and crowd. But before it touched a second aeroplane appeared like a speck in the clouds. It rushed down with extraordinary rapidity, in sharp dipping planes; hovered, as if looking for its prey, swooped at the tower on the station, and with extraordinary audacity wheeled twice above it in exquisite descending spirals. The flight of the first had brought a crowd of soldiers and Civic Guards on to every salient roof, and the circling challenge of the pursuer was followed by a regular salvo of musketry.

For a second it wavered: I could see the wings riddled with bullets. Then it steadied, dipped for a rush, and soared away magnificently over the surrounding heights.

Two minutes later the first aviator emerged from the station, a distinguished-looking white-moustached French officer, clearly in a fearful temper at the wrecking of his machine by the over-zealous Guards. To make quite sure of some one, they had raked his descent also with roof practice!

Hardly had the crowd quieted, when there

came another rush. Two fine-looking German officers, in the uniform of the famous " Death's Head " Hussars, were raced up under guard to the station. The crowd, with the remarkable restraint that is distinguishing the Belgians, watched their transference in complete silence. They had been brought from the north, where a German column has to-day cut all communication with Brussels.

For two hours this morning we heard the sound of cannon. Armoured cars, fitted with mitrailleuse wheels, have been running through the town. There have been also several mitrailleuses drawn by the famous dog-teams that can get up any hill-side.

No trains are running. The station is full of weeping women and children, who came yesterday to see their soldier husbands.

The motor-cars stand in their ready ranks, along the river-side. The Government purchased 12,000 at the start of the war from garages and private owners. Their use has changed the whole conditions of transport. The chauffeurs were sleeping in them. I had breakfast this morning with five of them in a little restaurant. A small boy gave me his Belgian badge. " If you get out alive," said his father, " our colours at least will have been rescued from the Germans."

(Namur had now become almost impossible for a stranger. The guns could be heard bombarding the distant forts. There was every chance that delay would mean being shut up for a siege, with no chance of getting news out, in which fortune had so far favoured me. Only a miracle—and Léon—had kept my car from being commandeered. I arranged to run out at dawn on Wednesday, and if the Germans were across the road on the north, to loop west by Charleroi and take our chance with the French army.

In the last evening I made an excursion on foot out of the town on the north, and, clear of the fortifications, had proof of the French being engaged in the direction of Gembloux. This confirmed the hope that the junction with the Belgian army had been made in time, and that the Germans would be forced to fight, against an army in position, in that region.)

NAMUR AND FRENCH LINES

Wavre, Wednesday.

I have just reached here from Namur—now a city of rushing crowds and anxious waiting.

All through Monday night the French were pouring into Namur, detraining outside the town. They were concealed under provision bags, etc., from the aviators. By day or twilight they arrived with helmets and cuirasses masked. The Spahis and Turcos had a warm welcome. Even a low cheer from the silent crowds, that washed from point to point like a restless sea.

All Tuesday morning, too, the fresh Belgian 4th Army Corps moved in and through, to replace and reinforce the well-tried 3rd. In the evening the officers dined and took coffee in the square; to speed off in motors later to their posts. There was even a little music and singing in the hotels. The Belgians know their anxious, lonely task is almost over. The rest they will face in good company.

This morning we came out, probably only just in time to escape the siege. Later, the Uhlans were across the line and road. A dispatch carrier was found shot by the roadside an hour after we passed.

Meanwhile the allied armies would seem to have been taking position in a vast semicircle from Diest to Namur, curving by Quatre Bras and Wavre. They have been choosing their ground. Not Waterloo this time—that is too close to the possible distractions in Brussels— but on a splendid field. It is broken ground, veiling the strength from the enemy.

Yesterday the long line of troops, drawn gradually in, stiffened. An engagement took place near Gembloux. The Uhlans were hunted back by the Cuirassiers. I was out near in the evening on foot, north of the city, and heard the operations going on.

Taking advantage of the lull, we got out of Namur early this morning, taking cross roads and lanes in front of the French and Belgian lines, and dodging the Germans.

The French were advancing, pushing the Germans back. We were soon involved. The face of the fields and low hills near Sombreffe was alive with moving troops—columns of cavalry, light guns moving into position, long snakes of infantry scattered up and down the wooded slopes. An extraordinary sight in the sun, among woods and trees.

We worked back through the lines. The deserted châteaux were occupied by various headquarter staffs. Occasionally the country and the closeness of troops opened. We ran among patrols of the light-blue Hussars. Anxious to get us out of the way, they passed us on courteously, with an occasional " arrest." They were clearing the last Uhlans, the remnants of those which were dispersed yesterday.

An officer warned us in a lane on a hill. " Wait here," he said. " We have run down some Uhlans in those woods." We waited half an hour. No movement, sunny fields ; nothing to be seen. Then suddenly, over a field, out of the wood, a rush of four horsemen, and the snap of a few shots from the far side. The next instant a running report of invisible rifles. Three horses fell. The fourth man fell from his saddle, and was dragged through the stubble. One of the other three got up, leaving his horse, walked a few paces, and fell. A grim sight in the summer fields.

Finally we were shepherded through to Mazy. Here we were blocked for two hours by advancing columns, Belgian guns and French cavalry. Slowly through the village (no peasants or children showing now!) filed regiment after regiment of French cavalry—glorious fellows. With their dulled, glimmering cuirasses, helmets covered in dust-coloured linen, and long black manes brushing round their bronzed red-Indian faces, they are peculiarly savage-looking, in a splendid sort of way.

Some had slight wounds, scarf-bound; a few the remains of the garish flowers, given them in some cottage last night, still stuck in their breast-plates. Several were pallid from loss of blood. All covered with dust and their horses foam-flecked.

As they passed, four abreast, some of the files were singing together. The singing was subdued and hoarse, from tired throats. The sound had a curiously wild, barbaric note. I remember nothing like it except the beginnings

of the Dervish chant, or the short moan of the
Indian war-song. They all had the stern, fighting
set of the face, the eyes sullen and looking only
at the distance.

A few glanced round and smiled grimly:
the sudden gleam of teeth and the flash of light
in the eye, breaking through the mask of bronze,
redness and dust, had a startling, almost shocking
effect.

The majority had no glance for us; set faces
and a rustle and stir of black, rusty plumes as
the horses shifted uneasily at the car.

Now and again officers, and white-moustached
colonels. A few noticed us, and gave various
orders. Two general officers were specially
noticeable in their subdued glint of armour.
The one, white-bearded, slightly bent, but with a
hawk's eye and a perfect seat and a great brown
Irish hunter. The other like a Viking, with a
white, drooping moustache. After inquiry of
one of his staff, he rode up as he passed, with a
dignified slight inclination. " You may pass on,
sir : Englishman—and friend," he said.

A line of Belgian artillery ; then the lighter

horses and trappings of Lancers; finally cyclists and a detachment of the Red Cross and ambulance.

They all passed up the lanes, out on to the hills, with a sort of rustling, intent silence; for there are no drums or music in this war.

For many of these great bronzed men, with here and there a fierce negroid African, we were the last link with the life of towns and civilians. A few hours, perhaps a day or so, of the sight of the stir of troops, of the empty country and the sound of war, and they will be lying in the long nameless trenches in the fields, with the harrow already passing over them.

South of Namur also the French are advancing across the Meuse, pushing forward on the offensive. There may soon be a straight diagonal of the Allies from Maastricht to Belfort.

The Belgians are waiting quietly, and, now, more confidently.

CHAPTER V

Louvain and Waterloo

THE encounter with the French regiments was reassuring for the time; but as I returned north of Wavre, it became again doubtful whether the link had really been made. News of the steady flood of Germans pouring by Diest upon Louvain met me near Brussels. To get an idea of the relative pace of the German advance I determined to return that night towards the Belgian left wing and discover for myself, if possible, the chances of its holding out.

A few hours at Brussels about noon were enough to convince me that it would be well now to keep outside and moving independently. The atmosphere of calm which the admirable organisation of the town had preserved so long, even in face of the near approach of the German cavalry on the south-east, was beginning to break down. The mistaken policy of silence was having its inevitable effect. For want of news, rumour was spreading. The Germans were said to be twenty miles, fifteen miles, ten miles away. Treat people as children, which has been the policy of the authorities in this war, and you will force them in the end to behave as children. If ever a population deserved to be taken into confidence it was that of Brussels. But it was now being treated with less and less trust every day. Papers were being suppressed; official communications grew less frequent and more obviously doctored. Our own authorities contributed by a curt request that all British correspondents should be ejected. How undeserved this was I was able, as not of the profession, to appreciate. In view of what was common knowledge, as to plans, positions and news, among scores of British correspondents in Brussels, their tact and loyalty were deserving of high praise and increased rather than diminished confidence.

I moved my base, therefore, to Waterloo, to a friendly little hostelry that had already proved

useful on our long skirmishing runs. In the
late afternoon another excursion to the south-
east left little doubt that the main German
advance was progressing on this northern line.
Reports of German cavalry met us in the villages. But what was happening to the Allied
armies? On the return I met, and followed
for some distance through the lanes, a regiment
of French infantry, who were making a forced
march to join the Belgians. It hardly seemed
possible, therefore, that the evacuation rumours
which I had heard in Brussels could be true.

To help towards a solution I started again,
this Wednesday evening, towards Louvain, and
ran through the town at dusk.

I had come to know Louvain very well, in
the days of my interviews with the Headquarter
Staff. There was a little restaurant at the
corner of the odd-shaped " Place," facing the
magnificient Hotel de Ville, where I could watch
the constant stream of cars and columns passing
in and out of the cordon that surrounded the
church, which contained the Commander-in-
Chief, and sometimes even the King. Occasion-

ally a British Staff officer would cheer me with the sight of the well-known uniform. There were always Belgian army surgeons, in the brown cap, ready for a gossip, restless horses with unhandy recruit riders, for amusement, and walks through the deserted picturesque streets, for a change to the eye. In a week or so I got to know it well, its quaint atmosphere of a mediæval university town charged with the restless electricity of military occupation, the uneasy mystery of an uncertain fate. And in another week or so—it was not.

I passed through it, or rather round it that evening for the last time; past the lines of soldiers sleeping under the station shelters, and the sentries with their handkerchief puggrees. I saw it only once again, the next night, by the glare of a few burning houses on the outskirts, beacons of the Belgian retreat and the German occupation.

Wednesday.

Beyond Louvain progress in the dark was very difficult. I failed to get the news I sought, but I heard something of the enemy. I made my way during the night down behind the Belgian lines at Geet Betz, with a returning officer as guide.

Here the advanced German right wing, chiefly cavalry—Uhlans and dragoons—has been trying to turn the Belgian left.

They have been repulsed once to-day in the attempt to cross the river, and suffered enormously owing to their advance in column formation.

The Belgians, too, have suffered considerably from the mitrailleuse, but have held their entrenchment with remarkable courage.

The Germans returned to the attack, and were expected to renew the assault to-night.

It was too dark to see or be seen in the undulating fields, but voices from the trenches and the movements of horses, and the occasional rush of a military motor, acted as signs.

Taking the chance of something happening within hearing, I made myself comfortable under some bushes near an open track leading through the lines of entanglements—so far as they could be located. There was an occasional sound of distant firing, outposts skirmishing;

later in the night a single whistle and the sound
of wheels grinding on tracks. What may have
been a battery moved up on to a rise in the
ground—seen as a shadow—about a quarter of
a mile to the south. Here they seemed to stop,
for there was silence again.

Another long wait, and then the sound of
cantering horses—some four or five—coming
by the track from behind, inside the lines.
Were they friends ?

They had passed me, and were in a line with
the slight hill to the south, when little sparks
of flame—half a dozen or so—glinted for a second
out of the shadows.

There was the slight " phit " of bullets through
the leaves, and then the purr of a maxim.
The canter broke into a sharp gallop down the
track, following upon a single shouted order.

Some heavier piece of ordnance coughed a
short distance to the left. A reply came from
far in front. A rattle, or rather an uneasy stir
and crackle, like a wet bonfire, moved along the
lines, and died away in the dark to the south.

The sound of the horses' feet stopped—

probably they had turned on to softer field-mould. And then silence again.

But this time the sense of human presence stayed with me. The darkness seemed strained and alive with tense expectancy.

The nights are short, and their cover shorter.

I had to be content with only the sound-picture of the night skirmish.

During the darkest hours before dawn we got back to Waterloo. On the southern edge of the battlefield itself I lay in the open, waiting for daylight, and listening for the sound of cannon commencing that should declare whether the Allies had really advanced, and were occupying some position that might still save Brussels and Belgium.

Waterloo, Thursday Morning.

A Shakespearean interlude this in the great Tragedy. Pistol, and Bardolph—what you will: the old story of the talkative coward!

I have come up here, for the first hours of quiet in three weeks; to escape from the constant excitement of wondering whether the next pair of galloping lancers approaching across the fields are friend or enemy; to avoid the agitated nerves of towns, where nine-tenths are spending their time in trying to discover whether there is any truth or personal bearing in what the last tenth lets them grudgingly know.

With all consideration for the necessity of secrecy, the thing is being overdone. No one can be got to believe that there is really no war going on; and for want of proper information imagination is beginning to run riot and nerves to snap.

A little company of peasants, fine, independent, sturdy folk, now safe behind the great lines of armies. A jolly company, full of joke and laughter, but with an eye all the time on the distant hill of the great battlefield.

And one stout, serious leader of the local Civil Guard, who spends each night beside the lion on the mound. Not alone; for three blue-bloused peasants with muskets wait at the other corners: a curious recall of the Great Duke's statue at Hyde Park Corner!

The last time I was here the three, aided by four girls, with their hair still down, from the farm, plotted against the braggart's peace. He dare not climb the 100-foot mound alone in the dark. But he wanted straw, for a warmer seat.

In his short absence the three others were hidden in a barn by the girls. The door shut. In the dark, alone, the leader set out to climb the mound, thinking they had gone on.

He talked loudly to himself. Then he began to call their names, " Pierre ! Jean ! Georges ! —GEORGES ! " He reached the top to find himself alone with the lion and the stars.

A wild yell: the two barrels discharged in panic: a head over heels descent: and a huge roar of laughter from the men and girls who had crept out into the road, prolonged till it became the hysteria of overtried nerves.

Then, the growl of cannon in the far distance, and all suddenly were silent.

Unwilling to precipitate, by my night attack, the arrangements of the peasants for escaping by their windows if the wandering Uhlans arrive, I have come down the battlefield to sleep, in a coat, under the stars.

FROM THE TRENCHES

The night is extraordinarily still. Twice the cannon have droned for a short time far off. A nearer shot, that roused a momentary shouting and movement in the sleeping village behind me, must have come from some nervous or sleepy Civil Guard.

Earlier in the night there were lights winking far away, towards Genappe; probably French contingents signalling.

And the meteors have been falling, criss and cross, in the summer warm darkness, over the darker cloud above the waiting armies to the east.

1815; and what were the men then thinking who lay rolled up in their cloaks to sleep their last night on the fields about me?

Ninety-nine years; and what are the still greater hosts of young and old men thinking, as they lie in their coats watching those same stars, only a few miles away from me, just behind that darker band of trees?

A century! And the only difference, that the one great army, that then faced up these slopes against us, now lies protecting us; in its turn ringing off a hostile army that then slept and stood with us as friends.

A century of progress! And what to show for it? The armies of four nations slightly shifted in their relation to these great plains, like spokes on a turning wheel.

Firing has recommenced, very faintly, in the distance. Not more disturbing than the harsh cry of a night-jar in the wood beside me.

For these few hours the terrible, unreal atmosphere of war, when every inch of earth threatens a surprise, and no moment seems real till it is past, has been absent. Night, and the stars, and quiet, have seemed like old friends, renewing a quiet of thought, restoring proportions.

I have been writing by the light of matches, under a coat.

Now the stir of wind before the dawn has passed. A few dogs are barking. And a shout or two tells of the Civil Guard changing their watchmen.

I can see to write in the grey dawn. Beyond my feet, out there on the hills, brain and sinew are again alert, and plotting cunningly to kill.

FROM THE TRENCHES

How much of hope and life and promise may have ended in darkness before the next night covers this sudden glow of sun ?

The uncertain outlines of the Waterloo monuments, commemorating heroic deeds of the past, in the grey half light have a sinster look. How soon will the sordid squalor of these new fights be in its turn converted into such memorials, to entrap new generations into dreaming that there is glory in war ?

CHAPTER VI

The Last of Brussels. The Flight, and the Flood

THURSDAY saw the ending of doubt. Although we did not know it, the floodgates were already opening; the Belgian army was retiring upon Antwerp, fighting only a gallant rearguard action at Louvain. The French advanced force, with its tentative claw outstretched towards Louvain, was beginning to wheel back rapidly to avoid leaving its flank exposed. Brussels was uncovered; and through the opening between the armies the torrent of grey troops was beginning to pour.

With the first light we made a circle towards Sombreffe, and came upon some retiring French cavalry. It was a puzzling spectacle, as at Waterloo we had not yet heard of the rapid change in the situation.

95

FROM THE TRENCHES

It should have been a quiet day. A quiet wandering through picturesque lanes, well behind the supposed fighting lines of the armies.

Running up and down the wooded, sunny lanes, on the stone setts, we even came as a relief to the bored peasant guards, lounging in their blue blouses, under straw shelters. At one remote village, high placed and only seemingly attainable by cobbled steep lanes, the Burgomaster made a solemn procession down the steps, with all the civic dignitaries, to meet us. They may have been waiting in session for a passer-by since the war began!

So we came down to Wavre; a short time ago filled with troops, now only empty, with an uneasy crowd at the corners, and a shifting swarm at the Mayoralty. We passed cheerfully out on the big, shaded road to Namur, confident of good passage.

The feeling changed, in the odd way it does in the most peaceful scenery when the war atmosphere touches it. The instinct for it is a valuable one in roving in "open" territory. With

THE LAST OF BRUSSELS

a rush down the road came a cyclist, wearing a tweed cap. Behind him, 300 yards off, from behind the trees, stepped a grey-uniformed Uhlan officer, who examined us through his glasses. The cyclist shouted, "There are seventeen up there behind the trees. I bade them good morning, and they didn't answer; so I said it was hot, and the officer said, 'Ouaai.' There's a car just beyond with bullet-holes in it, empty by the road." Lèon turned in a second on the broad road. The officer stepped back behind the trees. A rifle bullet spattered on the macadam; and we careered back to Wavre with the cyclist hanging on behind.

The news made little disturbance at the Mairie; orders had clearly been given. The Civil Guards were shut up on the top of the Town-hall; and all but the road-checks deprived of gun and sword. Six soldiers who remained were despatched in a car in the opposite direction. For the first time I began to realise that the country was to be evacuated—and without warning!

The guns were booming steadily from the

97

east, over Jodoigne. This was our direction. We started out again; but we were hardly out of the town, past some elaborate barriers, when straggling peasants began to meet us, crying that the Prussians were close in the woods; cavalry had been seen moving up the hills on either side.

It could scarcely be true; Wavre ought to be behind our lines, and we ought to be all right. We went slowly along the road, to make our peaceful character plain. I remember few more thrilling journeys than the slow mile along under the woods, keeping civilian hat and pipe prominent, and watching, without seeming to inspect, the close impending line of woods above the road.

So we came to the next village, Gastouche. The peasants were trickling out of the cottages, driving cattle hurriedly, dragging babies and bundles. A few gallant Civil Guards, rather pallid, but full of spirit, stood at the barriers. We ran gently through the village, reassuring where we could, turned a wide corner, and there, sitting by the road, leaning on their horses, were a squad of about twelve Uhlans! They were some 200 yards off.

I could not make sure of the uniform for the moment; so, to cover the retreat of the car, I walked a few paces towards them and looked through the glasses. In reply, a Uhlan stepped out and lifted his. I let him have a good look, to confirm my pacific appearance, and then walked slowly back. The car was already out of sight, ready round the corner. We swirled back through the village, hurrying the inhabitants. Then, at the far end, leaving the car ready up a lane, we mounted a bank, and watched the troop ride in, pull down the flag, and cut the wires.

Picking up all the women we could, we were back in Wavre to give the news. Nothing could be done. Not a friendly soldier seemed alive in the neighbourhood. For a time we watched. With half a dozen anxious elders I laboriously climbed the great church tower, We strained our eyes, to see nothing real, but a lot of imaginary conflagrations. Meanwhile the guns boomed far off, and the refugee villagers began to pour in below us. A curious, pathetic sight. The women had put on their best black dresses, to save them; the men, their black coats. Later, they came in as they were, dragging and carrying children, women just from or near childbirth, girls with scarfs full of food or apples. They were frightened, hurrying, and quiet. But when the town at last understood the rage of the men, and of the women too, is past description. There was no outcry, but they cursed, clustering together, some of the men in tears, at being deprived of arms, at not being allowed to defend their homes—they, a horde of big men, against a handful. They were long past reasoning with. It was a sane order that deprived even the Guards of arms and shut them, chafing, behind the communal steps.

At last the sight of the refugees grew too painful. We went off to pick up what we could. Twice we ran to the near end of Gastouche, bringing back untidy loads of children and mothers. The second time we tried to get through, by a corner, a few miles further to Overrysche. We had just passed the barrier of faggots and village carts, with two nervous-bold Guards at the " present," when at the end of a short cross lane through the cottages on the right I saw the flicker and movement of horse soldiers passing, sixty yards off.

The same instant a shot came from a cottage behind them, and a rush of shrieking women down the lane. We turned at once and waited: the Uhlans, some eight of them, had wheeled back out of sight, where the cottages ran into the wood. The men shouted to the women to keep indoors ; a few stray children ran back and forwards in the lane, crying. Then the door of a far cottage opened, and the crippled soldier who had fired the shot was half-carried out. A fine red-bearded fellow. He was perspiring, inarticulate with rage at having missed and with the lust of fighting. We shoved him into the car, with a few more women, and got back to Wavre. As we passed, we saw some thirty of the Civic Guard shut in a yard, down a lane, behind a wooden barrier.

Even the civic calm had begun to quiver.

FROM THE TRENCHES

The surging, homeless crowd of villagers were talking loudly at the corners; and every now and then a farmer in shirtsleeves bicycled furiously in, to complain of a house occupied or horses stolen. The German outposts were all round us, and the place undefended.

The utterly helpless agitation of a population unable to do anything, seeing itself, without an hour's notice from the authorities, forced to surrender home after home, and forbidden to resist, was an inexpressibly painful sight, and cannot occur often, even in war. Undefended towns, when abandoned, generally have some warning. Here the enemy dropped out of the sky in an hour; and the peasants looked round to find their own army gone. There was not even the previous " working up " of a losing fight.

A shout and a rush. A cyclist, red-flushed, raced into the square, brandishing a Uhlan helmet, picked up—who knows where ? Another greater shouting and swarming, and two stout farmers rode in, leading four splendid Uhlan horses, Irish-bred, and full of mettle. Where

THE LAST OF BRUSSELS

did they come from ? What did it all mean ?
Time may show.

Waterloo, Thursday night.

To-day's story is still unfinished.

As the day wore on at Wavre, it became clear
that Brussels was to be included in the general
evacuation. The sound of the guns could be
followed, as the Belgians fell back towards
Antwerp.

This was, then, no more a matter of " Uhlan-
hunting," by withdrawal and encircling movement. The Prussians had penetrated too far,
by surprise or with foreknowledge ; the country
was being evacuated.

The horses of Uhlans captured were fresh,
signifying no lost or wandering parties, but
portions of a main column that had camped
near. The troops, also, which we had seen were
behaving quietly, not in the savage manner of
the after-fight. They knew the country was
clear of soldiers, and could take their time.
To this, probably, we owed our own immunity
at Gastouche. A column of some eight hundred

horse could be seen with the glass moving over the hills south of Wavre.

We heard that Louvain was being evacuated. About five o'clock we left the Civil Guard behind their railings, helpless and furious, and hurtled towards Brussels. To some twenty little patrols of cavalry and cars we gave the news. Their faces told me it was not the unexpected.

Not a quiet run. Twice the distant " burr " of the aeroplanes, and we identified the German " Taube " machines over the woods. We turned east towards Jodoigne ; to find the trenches empty, our army gone. An armoured car, packed with German infantry, flashed through a cross-road behind us. Once again a waving of arms checked us, and the peasants, half fearful, half excited, warned us of a wood ahead ; but we rushed it without incident.

So back to Brussels—to the close gathering of restless crowds under the lamps, the quick glance of suspicious eyes, and rumour, nervous, whispered rumour.

The roads were crowded with fugitives with

bundles, cows, and carts. The suburbs hummed uneasily. The evening papers were just appearing, announcing that " the situation is unchanged ; the Germans are still along the Meuse " ; while every third man on the road had seen them within fifteen miles, and the air had quivered with the approaching guns all day !

The game of secrecy has been played too long. It has deceived nobody and increased the unrest. It is to be hoped that the good sense of the Belgians will forgive it, for the sake of its innocent purpose, when the hour of triumphant return comes.

I left Brussels again late in the evening and worked down towards Louvain, in the dark, meeting the last of the fugitive crowds and the trains of wounded. Leaving the car securely hidden, by by-lanes and cobble-ways I got forward, avoiding the flank of the retreating Belgians, and making for the light of two burning cottages—my last sight of Louvain.

A few small fights were still going on, as sound and sight indicated. Covering parties of Belgians, in small numbers, were heroically sacrificing themselves to protect the strategic retreat on its northward wheel.

Below a slight field-slope, upon the crest of which the flash of rifle fire and the long snake-rattle of the mitrailleuse showed where some section was still making a last stand, I found a shelter. I had made for the west of their certain line of retreat down the fields, and hid uncomfortably in a ditch of bushes, which discovered itself, accidentally and somewhat painfully, in the dark.

Clearly, only a few men were holding the trench above. The whistle of shot, well overhead and to my left, was continuous. Soon there was the buzz of a motor down an invisible lane below, and one of the German cars, fitted with a mitrailleuse-wheel, got into position, to begin raking them from the rear. By means of motors, in this flood of advance, the Germans have moved up light guns and infantry at the speed of cavalry.

A few scattered shots getting nearer told me that the men above me were running back. One, blundering so that I could hear his feet, clearly wounded, stopped running, as the sound showed, near me. I got him after a time into the same ditch as myself. It ran along close to where he fell.

Having cleared this corner, the Germans had evidently something better to do. The firing above and below stopped. After a long wait I managed to get the little trooper, one of a regiment I had chatted with last week, down to an abandoned cottage in the lane below. Only an arm wound; so I left him, bandaged, for the Red Cross to fetch in.

I got back slowly, keeping the line by the burning cottages. The drive that followed will not easily be forgotten—at headlong speed through awkward lanes. Only once—we were running without lights—did a challenge stop us; but we chanced its being a friend, and only heard the stray shot after us, in the dark.

Some day I may be able to write the story of the "audacious chauffeur." He swept me thirty miles through the night with extraordinary nerve and skill. Only one of several daring runs.

There was no rest this last night. It was

clear Brussels would be occupied in a few hours. In that event we were under promise to bring out a certain frightened mother and her babies. The event had seemed remote; but, like the tide on flat sands, while we watched the distant edge of the sea, it was already up, round, and behind us.

We were already all but cut off, since Brussels must now in a few hours cut the last of its communications.

Friday, Daylight.

Down the car went again at 3 a.m., while I tried to get some sleep. It seemed only a moment later that there was shouting in the village, and a rattle of wooden sabots passed under the window, running.

I looked out, under the cottage blind; and in a few minutes, through the grey early light, two or three mounted, grey-shimmering Lancers walked their horses down the street. It seemed as if they were provoking the cottagers to fire at them. More probably they were perfectly confident in the general evacuation of this district.

THE LAST OF BRUSSELS

There were more, the women told me later, riding past outside the cottages.

It was an undignified time of waiting, with no chance of a fight. Nothing to do but dress, smoke, and get the papers ready in case they came in. The terrible " game " is so real, even for the non-fighter, that their passing, and the quiet of the empty street that followed, brought more relief than one cares usually to confess to.

Bruges, Friday noon.

It was no use trying to sleep there, with the nervous chatter beginning of the women clustered under the windows, and with the chance of " more " coming. The loan of a captured Uhlan horse, a trophy which the village was now anxious to dispense with, and another lift from a car returning for wounded, took me down again in the fields to the east of Brussels.

A different sight this morning. For the Prussians were already half-way into Brussels, on a clear parade march. The squalor and horror of the battlefields were behind them. They were flooding easily through open, still country, with the surrender of the city already promised them. The insane game of war was being played out with at least one cleanly, if, for us, melancholy, move.

I got out short of Cortinbeck. A few casual cyclists gave me confidence to wait. The roads were moving in the distance with advancing cavalry. I could see, with the glasses, more crossing the sky line. It seemed better to avoid, on the return, some dusty advance party patrols, in cars ; but they appeared to be paying civilian casuals little attention.

When I regained the outskirts of Brussels the entanglements of wire and the barriers of omnibuses were being cleared away—that pleasantly reassuring joke—and the arms of the Civil Guard were being piled by the streets. Zealous, honest Dogberries ! It seemed hard that, after being a conscientious and needful nuisance to their friends for so long, they should not be allowed to challenge or scrutinise even one enemy !

I did not wait to see the entry into Brussels. There are limits to the passive endurance even

THE LAST OF BRUSSELS

of a non-combatant. The only triumphant entry I shall willingly witness is the return there of the brown, tired, gay-hearted little Belgian soldiers, whom I have learned to admire as an army and sympathise with individually in their magnificent struggle against odds.

The nature of our load made it wise to make a safe circuit west of Brussels, on our retreat. The watching lion at Waterloo, as we passed, seemed to wear a different look: surprised to see no battle array, indignant at his desertion.

At first, by request, we did courier work, carrying the news to isolated town-garrisons. The further we got, the less curious did the people become for news. Resignation, apathy, stolid village optimism, according to the locality.

Our armfulls of blue-eyed babies, five, six, and eight, brought the only smiles to the faces we saw. The great mass of cars had already gone; yesterday and before. A few hurrying cars, carts, and bicycles with luggage. Now and again in a village the little crowds of peasant fugitives with bundles. Occasionally some women, resting and cooking by the wayside.

111

FROM THE TRENCHES

The further down the line, the more troublesome again became our familiar checks, the local watchmen, at their now pathetically futile barriers. It would have been cruel to assure them, when they became obstructive, that their authority was gone. We circled by Waterloo westward, almost as far as Oudenarde.

At one village a swarm of little dark-eyed Flemings, in sabots, pretended to shoot us with large bows and arrows made of half-hoops, from behind a sham barrier of branches and wheel-barrows; a half-tragic commentary. At Ghent our car was within a single word of being "requisitioned." The babies fulfilled their object by capturing smiles and safe passage.

At Bruges we have been kept for an hour because "German spies" have been signalled as having passed in a car up the road. Having got so far as to stop all the bridges, the dignitaries can do no more. The world is upset, and must wait.

Ostend, Friday night.

The crowd of carts and cars that accumulated

112

at last proved too much even for the patience of the Gardes, and we all crushed through and over.

Nowhere had the news been received; everywhere the blind is still kept-down. It is a dangerous game to play, with men raging as I have heard them the last few days. But the result may justify it.

It is no good recalling the shadow moments of pain and tragedy that cover like a cloud even the small corner which one man may see of this destruction and panic called war.

Every event is out of proportion, impossible. The dead body one stumbles over is no more real or important than the bad-mannered shopkeeper who is doing his best as a civic sentinel. One thinks of nothing but the chance of the next fantastic incident; and if it comes as a death or as a child crying, it seems equally serious, equally foolish, equally without origin or relation to the next event.

In the course of these two days, started so peacefully, it will be seen that we have been involved in the French retreat on the west, in the Prussian flood and the dramatic evacuation in the centre, in a corner of the last battle at Louvain, on the east, in the evening, the morning entry of the enemy to occupy Brussels, and finally in the east of the flight to the south. If we put the facts of the last few days together, so far as we know them, without going outside official information, this seems to be about the position :

The German northern army, profiting perhaps even more than we did by the check at Liége, had two possible alternatives, supposing their objective to be Brussels, and the " hole " on the frontier by Mons and Charleroi. And Brussels was necessary, to re-affirm their credit in Berlin.

The first alternative was through by Gembloux, Quatre Bras, and Genappe, avoiding the forest of Soignes. This would have struck the weak link between the French advanced force, in the neighbourhood of Sombreffe, and the Belgian lines from Wavre to Diest.

The second was to push north, along the frontier, {to Hasselt, and break through the Belgian left before it could be reinforced by the French, threatening both Antwerp and Brussels.

This was their choice. They were aware that the French could not push up rapidly enough to establish the link firmly, or in great enough numbers to be able to reinforce the menaced left wing.

The French, nevertheless, did some very fine marches in order to profit by the splendid Belgian resistance at Liége and Haelen. But it was too late for the change of plan. When I was among them, at Mazy and Gembloux and Perwez, it seemed as if they were in time to force the Germans to take the more southerly line, and face them and the Belgian arc on their north. The Germans knew better. Under screen of their scattered Uhlans, here and there all over the country, forcing the Belgians, always in inferior numbers, to expand and contract as their attacks were located, they moved a far larger force than was estimated across the Meuse. Behind their pause at Liége they converted the hastily mobilised inferior troops, whom the Belgians had learned to despise, into the engine of magnificent equipment and pace that is now launched across Belgium.

This has pushed rapidly north, by motor, ahead of the French ; and by sheer weight of numbers, hurling columns in mass, at great sacrifice of life, has broken the Belgian left at Diest and Aerschot in the terrific fights of the last two days.

The French made great efforts to get up, and actually got a certain number by forced marches far enough to take the places of decimated Belgian regiments in the line. But the smashing numbers and artillery made the Belgian position, in its open trenches and entanglements on easy country, impossible. Their left once turned, the small Belgian army had no choice but to fall back on Malines and Antwerp. They had to choose between defending Brussels, to keep the link with the French, and covering Antwerp, which opened the road to Brussels. Antwerp was obviously the more important, and better prepared for defence. Brussels must have been destroyed in a siege, with immense loss of life to the huge numbers who have swarmed into it.

Wavre and all the district where I was travelling to and fro yesterday was therefore evacuated, as the Belgians retired north. Their retirement compelled a synchronous falling back of the French upon the Sambre, to protect their own left wing when the link with the Belgians was broken.

The Germans obtained free passage both on the east and south to Brussels. The rapidity of their progress is evidenced by the fact that when I passed round west of Brussels to-day, advance cavalry patrols were already reported in the neighbourhood of Oudenarde (about 30 miles west of Brussels, towards Lille).

It will be seen that, on paper at least, the Belgian army is in no pleasant position. If the Germans continue to press northward on their left flank, the Belgians will constantly have to be wheeling to their own left front, to face them on the east. They will be forced to retreat until they rest upon Malines and Antwerp.

At the same time any small force of Germans

left in Brussels is largely out of the game. The Belgians threaten their northern communications. The farther the Germans push north, to Ghent or Ostend, the more danger that their lines can be cut. All depends whether this German northern advance is merely an army of occupation, to subdue Belgium, or the main army of advance upon France. In the latter case, it will not now be stopped this side of the frontier.

Ostend, Saturday night.

To-day the German flood has advanced with extraordinary rapidity. The Belgian army is for the moment off the board. At express speed and with clockwork regularity the country is being occupied. We know now that this must be the main army of attack.

Sweeping from the east by three routes, and through and past Brussels, the main German advance has turned south-west. Passing close to Waterloo and through Hal it is directed against the frontier between Valenciennes and Maubeuge. A lighter cavalry column is passing further north, as if towards Lille.

THE LAST OF BRUSSELS

The main advance, since my encounter with it at Cortinbeck and at Waterloo, on the morning after the battle of Louvain and Aerschot, it has been impossible to follow. But to-day I took the region from the French frontier, on the west of Brussels, with some idea of "beating all the bounds" of what is left of our surrendered but unoccupied country. For, with the exception of the section from Malines to Antwerp, Belgium has been surrendered, the troops on the way have been disbanded, and the Civic Guard has been discharged. At Alost yesterday I met many of them, dismissed from Brussels, but still in uniform and anxious for news. To-day I came across them again in Ghent, further reduced and in mufti. In many cases their wives have insisted on destroying their uniforms.

I looked forward to a restful day in the Flemish rural districts, with, perhaps, some news of the French. I was tired of coming upon Uhlans round corners. It is a peculiarly trying business, exploring for an enemy, with no troops, no sound of guns, or the consequent rumours, to warn beforehand of their proximity! It is even more disagreeable when you have to lose your enemy again rather faster than you have found him !

The wandering about the fertile, remote province, with its long, shaded, cobbled roads and low-cottaged, dusty villages, was a pleasant change. In the morning the region was still entirely untouched by the war. The dark-eyed children, with bleached blonde hair, in noisy sabots, swarmed like puppies in the streets and about the car. The Civil Guard were the only distraction. In the country fields they generally could not read at all, and waved us on, blushing in their blue blouses. In the small towns they could read " Vlamsch," but no French, which irritated them. Often " Madame " had to be called in to help, before the carts and ploughs were shoved aside. One old peasant was particularly troublesome. He was both deaf and blind, and behind his road-barrier of harrows he nursed a rusty bayonet dating from Waterloo.

The only incidents of the early day were an agitated hay-cart that upset upon us, and a line of retreating engines, at Ingelmunster, which took the level crossing at the same moment as ourselves. "The service is so disorganised," the stationmaster excused himself for our scratched paint.

On the French frontier—near Poperinghe—we met our friends the French. A cavalry contingent entertained us pleasantly at lunch round the soup-pot. Satisfied of the safety of our western border, we turned east, to cut across the noses of any advancing German columns. My object was to discover if they were striking north to Ostend, or direct west towards Lille, as well as south-west on their main line. Through Ypres, Roulers, Vijve, and Deynze we ran to Ghent. The country was still clear; the "war feeling" absent; but the Flemish are slow to catch emotional infections.

In Ghent we met the news. The Germans had flooded incredibly swiftly north. A column had in the morning reached Melle, just south of Ghent. Reports of eye-witnesses of its passing put it at 70,000 cavalry. Clearly it was a fair-sized and fast column.

I felt certain that it would turn west, and not

continue north to Ostend. It must form part of a quick cavalry turning movement to the north of the main advance on the French and British position. We should have time to make certain later in the day. Passing quickly through Ghent, to avoid " requisitioning " of the car, we pushed out towards Termonde, on the east, hoping to be able to make sure of the position of the Belgian lines also, on their new arc of defence.

Warnings of " Uhlans " soon began to meet us in quick succession. We touched the outposts of the Belgians, and having thus made secure of our two frontiers, west and east, to avoid unnecessary risk we ran back to Ghent. The Belgians are worn and have lost heavily. The troops do not yet know where the British are. They were, consequently, difficult to deal with.

Ghent was in the now familiar condition of crowd panic. The railway communication had practically ceased. Disbanded soldiers were trying to get away. The squares were crowded with anxious, waiting people; the roads beginning to fill with the crowds of fugitives on foot and in carts. While waiting for a few moments to talk to Belgian friends—quickly made in time of war—occurred an unpleasing incident. A corporal of the line, followed by three privates in uniform, suddenly rushed across the square, their faces red and drawn with terror, and demanded the car. The chauffeur, an old soldier, was at once involved in fierce argument. My new-made friends faded away.

The crowd, simmering with panic and crying already of " treachery " and " revolution," as the effect of the extent to which they have been kept in ignorance of the military situation until too late, swarmed round in an instant angrily.

At the words " Give it up or I fire," frantically shouted, I thought it time to interfere. I had two bayonets at once thrust against my chest.

" Where do you wish to be taken, friend ? " He growled the name of some village on the French frontier. The position grew clearer. He was one of the " disbanded " escaping to his home. There were many, all about us, but in civilian clothes.

" I will take you, in uniform, to any place you choose at the front ; but no law compels me to carry fugitives." ("Fuyards" is much stronger.) "Get into clothes like mine, and I'll drop you at any (sacré) hiding-hole that suits you."

The effect on the crowd was electric. The soldiers faded; and we left, after a proper interval, to let the crowd cool down.

Not a quarter of a mile to the west of Ghent, where the roads were spotted with carts of escaping households, an enormous Franciscan monk blocked the road, with uplifted cross. "Stop, and take us, in the name of the Virgin." He was supporting two wounded soldiers. It appeared that, in foolish panic, all the private hospitals had been emptied. "Sauve qui peut" was the word. The sick and wounded soldiers, many from Liége, dressed in any odd civilian clothes, were being turned out on to the roads to find their way to remote homes.

We bundled them in; took them to the nearest railway line; flagged a train at a level crossing, and sent them off, with breathless blessings from the railway window. But the roads were full of them: men limping, men almost crawling, without money, and with only the dangerous soldier's " pass " to carry them to their villages, already held by the enemy.

For many hours we had given up our purpose of localising the column, and travel backwards and forwards over the province, scattering them far and wide in remote villages, either to their wives, or often in the care of kindly women, who would pretend to be their wives or mothers, in safer places. The strange panic feeling had now spread wide. Everywhere were the little swarms of subdued people, with puzzled, sullen faces, seen in forlorn villages. The cottages were emptying, shop-windows being hurriedly covered, and signs hastily painted out.

The Civil Guard, disbanded, were being confusedly shoved into civilian dress by their terror-stricken wives and daughters.

Occasionally I had to sit and make explanatory conversations in the market places to knots of depressed Flemish civic fathers, who would otherwise have made even more difficulty about our frequent journeyings. " Where are the English ? " " Who has betrayed us ? " " Why have we been kept in the dark, and now find ourselves helpless ? "—all of them unanswerable questions.

It became peculiarly difficult to keep up such talk, when, later in the day, every quarter-hour would come a rush of clogs down the street, and the roar of " They're coming ! " The elders melted miraculously, and I was left in the empty street facing a row of half-filled beer glasses, and the thought that it might be true this time.

Towards evening we ran into the French out-posts again, at Ypres. They are well over the frontier, and ready.

We turned north at last in the dark, realising that even in these few hours the tide of Germans had almost cut us off, even from the coast. No province was to be left us by the immense efficiency of the machine. It was moving now over undefended country. It has been notably revised since Liége.

But a cry from a dark group under the dark trees on a lonely twelve miles of road again stopped us : " *Nous avons peur* " (we are afraid) wailed sadly, as we shot past. Two wounded soldiers, with two children who had been to visit them. They, like many others, were from the heroic Liége forts. They would be safe at their homes in Courtrai. On the road, wandering, as many more were, right across the German line of advance, they were in considerable danger.

To run for Courtrai was to run from the French lines, directly at the head of the probable German advance.

Peasants, however, assured us that nothing had been seen; and it would complete our locating of the positions of all the armies in this corner of the world, if we found trace of the enemy.

It was an exhilarating night run. Still the knots of folk at the corners, but now even the children were silent.

We dropped them, our last load, at the cross road entering Courtrai. The car was turned to come back; when, from far down the other branch, towards Deynze, came the roar of a racing car at full speed, devouring the silence. Half a mile off sounded a shot, and again two, nearer us, a little later. We started to move, and in a few seconds a car with three Belgians in uniform rushed?past us. One lay back, and his arm was being bound up by his companion. They shouted warning. " They are back there : we have come over one." And again : " Look out ! There are more in front ! "

We did our best to keep up with them—a rather wild race in the dark, on roads straight but rough, for long black miles at a time. They drew ahead, but this served also to draw the fire from us. Twice again a shot sounded sharply in front. But we only had the half-gleam of the lamps on a shadow-man and a frightened shadow-horse, when we, in turn, passed the Uhlan patrols who had fired.

It was not worth continuing as far as the French lines, clearly the object of the car ahead. We turned off on the first good diagonal to the north. We had learned what we wished. These were the usual Uhlans clearing the ground ; ahead of an advance to the west ; not for the present to the north.

The return to Ostend all through the night was

strange in its quieter fashion. The Flemish peasant, once he is frightened or suspicious, becomes a dangerous man. We had serious difficulties at infinite numbers of barriers. And always the halt brought round a muttering, shuffling swarm of hostile faces and voices. Along the roads we passed small carts and wagons, creaking slowly with families of fugitives. There was no reason for any one to fly in view of the general surrender, but suspicion and panic were spreading, and stories of German savagery wildly exaggerated and widely believed.

Occasionally the lights glanced off long lines of black-shawled women, returning from night pilgrimages to more potent saints. In the middle of long black stretches of lonely road we passed suddenly before open shrines, blazing with votive tapers. Near big villages, in the larger shrines the heads of many children were silhouetted sharply against the dazzling altars. Generally a ring of kneeling women outside shut the children in; and the momentary sound of chanting came and went as we passed.

At a crossing a train, without lights, crept

back timidly towards Ghent. At another, seven trains in succession went past, full of volunteers shipped to the French frontier. A car, with the windows smashed by bullets, deserted under the trees, told of the passing of more Uhlans. We half expected to find the Uhlans already here when we returned; but it was only the exit of carts and carriages of luggage that interrupted our race in, near midnight. We had started to define the boundaries left to us, and before our return very little was left us but the sea!

England, Sunday.

Arriving at midnight at Ostend, I found myself " almost the very last " foreign inhabitant. The Uhlans had been reported at twenty miles; we had seen them at thirty; they were expected at any hour. Of the method of my leaving, and of the episode of the dramatic visit of the Fleet the next day, the time has not yet come to write.

The placid river under Rochester Castle, two days later, in very tranquil sunlight, is the last memory picture of this phase. The peace atmosphere of England hit the senses like a thick, pleasant vapour. The sensation was actually physical. I have experienced it again, at every subsequent crossing in or out of the countries at war.

CHAPTER VII

ANTWERP AND MALINES

THE passage of the great armies across the frontier and through eastern France could not be approached. For the moment, west Flanders, behind the German lines, offered no comfortable footing. There seemed a prospect, however, that Antwerp might be immediately besieged. My journey there was further justified by the chance of discharging a useful public mission. I started by Flushing; spent a day sailing with some Zeeland fishermen; and thence, as the railway to Antwerp was interrupted, completed the journey by boat and irregular transport.

Saint Nicholas, Friday.

Holland is friendly. There is only one opinion among the fishermen, sailors, and peasants of the south.

132

Picturesque fellows they are, with their black caps, mahogany faces, earrings, and gold brooches; and the women, with their white head-dresses, black silk wings, and brown necks and arms, with coral and gold bangles.

No doubt in their minds. 'Anything but the German flag! We'll stay as we are, if possible. If not, we'll be English for preference!'

The Dutch soldiers on the frontier take the same view: 'Any fate but Prussia!' But they have a fear: 'In other countries this is an officer's war; not of the people. Who knows what 'they' will decide up there! But, as far as we have a voice, no traffic with Germany!'—and then usually follows an anecdote concerning a recent civic snub to a member of the royal family, which need not be set out.

There is strong repudiation of the story that German troops have been allowed across Dutch Limburg: 'They were refugees, all who passed; and, of course, we welcome all such. Why, we even have the German Crown Prince's family at the Hague.' (This is generally believed!)

FROM THE TRENCHES

A Dutch fishing-smack, with an Irish skipper, put me across yesterday, Thursday, on to the south bank of the Scheldt. A warm sleepy sunset, and a drowsy peaceful little toy port.

A burst of warlike energy had carried the fishermen as far as the making of wire entanglements; but gaps, large enough for the passing of the stouter burghers, had been considerately left.

I travelled some distance on a goods truck. When it halted, a few idle, polite sentries, anxious to avoid responsibility, passed me on to a cavalry patrol. Pleasant, talkative fellows, they handed me over in turn, on the frontier, to a company of mounted Belgian volunteers with whom they had been fraternising.

These had as yet seen no fighting themselves; but there was only one subject of talk, the Highlanders: 'There are 20,000 of them, and they pipe all the time! At Mons they played while the rest shot, and the pipers can play with one hand and shoot with the other; it must be terrible!' I had this story ten times over.

And again, of the British: 'They are uncanny

fellows ! Why, even in hopeless positions on a
retreat they never go on retiring till they are
told to ! '

The patrol was without its officer. It is a
tragic little episode, illustrative of the conditions
of war. His mother was Dutch; and she lay
dying just across the frontier, in Holland. As a
Belgian officer, he could not cross to see her in
uniform or with arms, or he would be imprisoned.
If he crossed as a civilian, he would be treated as
a deserter. He was away, trying, in vain, to get
some relaxation of the laws governing neutral
territory. Only a mile or two off, and yet he
must be too late.

As no passenger train to Antwerp would leave
before next day, one of my new friends packed
me into a van, one of a long train of vans on
trucks going up with supplies to the front. The
intention was to join the main line at St. Nicholas,
and take the train thence in the morning to
Antwerp. But as the supply train ran on to
near Malines, there was every reason for going
with it.

A few of the Malines residents were creeping

back, in the dusk, to the empty town. The Belgians have shown remarkable pertinacity in these 'interval' returns. A father and son, sleeping in their cart on the road, gave me a lift into the town.

Malines was deserted. It was the night of an interval between the retirement of the Germans and the resumption of advance by the Belgians. But the German bombardment continued, directed obviously at the destruction of the church and the empty buildings. At intervals the guns resumed throughout the night; but their fire was ill-directed.

As we were threading our way through the streets, a clatter of hoofs warned us to take shelter. We hurried into the empty church. In the dark, through the door, we heard, and saw in the faint light, a few peasants walking past with hands raised, driven by some mounted Uhlans. Four of the peasants were left sitting hunched up on the steps. After long, anxious moments the patrol clattered away, firing wantonly at the windows of the church; and again firing in the distance.

ANTWERP AND MALINES

During our wait, to let them get clear away, there was the deafening report of a shell bursting not far from the church; and plaster rattled down from the roof.

Much of the town was in ruins; swaths through the houses, cleared away to free the fire from the Belgian forts. And the prominent buildings, public and private, had evidently provided targets for the German guns.

To-day I heard that, while I was getting clear of the town, a very gallant rescue was being made by four Belgian ambulance men. They ran cars to the river, crossed a small pontoon, left by the Germans, on foot, and succeeded in carrying eight wounded Belgians, left in a little schoolhouse behind the German lines, back across the pontoon to the cars. They had been lying there untended.

The Belgian troops, or what I saw of them as I worked back to the railway this morning, seemed in excellent heart. The repulse of the Germans two days ago, and the strength of the fortress behind them, have gone far to remove the anxiety that inevitably followed their heavy losses in the recent field actions and the growing consciousness of hopelessly inferior numbers.

Many of them belonged to the fresh divisions, the flower of the heroic little army. At last they know 'where the English are,' and 'what the French are doing,' and the vague and intimidating hugeness of their own task has contracted to a definite, perceptible plan of campaign.

An eye-witness tells me the retreat from Louvain was conducted in splendid order and in high spirits. The Germans followed till they came under the fire of the outermost fort.

To-day the little Belgians were as cordial and ready to smile as in the first days after Liége.

In the grey morning to-day the country near the Belgian lines was an extraordinary sight. Already the light was flashing from the water of slight, precautionary inundations; and there are whole tracts ready to follow suit. Chateaux destroyed, for purposes of defensive fire; woods cut down; trees, which obstructed the ranges, hacked away; a country already half devastated, as if by an enemy.

But the success outside Malines had reassured

the peasants. They could be seen dribbling slowly back to their cottages in unobtrusive clusters on road and field.

A troop train, crammed with soldiers sitting close on the floor of cattle-trucks, many of them of the volunteer army, brought me back towards the headquarters. Troops were constantly leaving us, and fresh truckloads being added : all in good heart, and full of individual exploits. We were banged about, and shunted here and there among guns and ammunition trains.

At one point the firing sounded only just across the field. The train stopped, and several trucks emptied in little coloured floods of soldiers into the wet fields. The men doubled in open order, just over the edge, out of sight through the green park-like trees in the sunlight. The scattered fire gradually drew away ; and we moved slowly on again.

Antwerp, Friday night.

At St. Nicholas, the headquarters of the General commanding on the west, I ran again into the uneasy, strained atmosphere of the towns near the fighting line. It was familiar at Namur and elsewhere. Uncertainty, constant coming and going, parade, spy-mania, secrecy, and military rule. In such places the civilian is like a child confused in the middle of a race-course; something to be herded and scuffled out of the way; suspicion of others is the only safe outlet for his panic feeling. We do not know this condition yet in England. May we never experience it ! To catch an eye is to create an enemy. A sudden movement brings a rush of the silent crowd. An outward routine; an inward volcano of fear, mistrust, and over-strained nerves.

The soldiers at the front, if one can get there, are friendly enough. Only for the moment, when men are going into, or are actually in action, does the ' war-mask ' make a man remote and unaccountable. Out of action the more humorous northerner drops it gladly; the southerner, less easily. Farther back from the front, at the anxious, waiting, military head-quarters, or in the town or village strung to snapping point of nervous tension by the immediate uncertainty and peril, is the danger-point for the looker-on. I made the experiment, as an obvious stranger, of sitting outside a restaurant. In five minutes a white-whiskered, respectable magistrate sat down opposite, and glared dangerously. "You are a renegade!" I made no answer. A crowd began to collect. "You are a German!" It was dangerous to let him go on. Better attract the police than risk the crowd. "You may have the right to question me, sir: you have none to insult me"—and I stood up suddenly, upsetting him behind the heavy little table. A regulation "arrest" followed; the first. In two hours I was interrogated seven times by different descriptions of uniformed and civilian officialdom; and three times was escorted to various military authorities, who, at last, became not unnaturally petulant. Finally I had to retire within doors. This is merely illustrative of the atmosphere; for the individuals remained undemonstrative.

Troop trains poured in and out of the station. Boy-sentries, struggling under huge rifles, paraded the cobbles and mustered at the corners.

FROM THE TRENCHES

At last, the single train to Antwerp. Nobody but inhabitants were allowed to enter by it. The " word of the day " was whispered me with infinite secrecy. The women, waiting to identify the wounded, who passed in constant groups from the trains, swarmed over the platform for farewells. Then a dark journey under a red moon ; a passing sight of camps, and soldiers moving without lights ; spaces of water.

And the end of it all, an easy, normal, almost careless passage into a comfortable town, sure of itself and its defenders. For Antwerp lives perfectly tranquilly. Only at night are the dark streets and the unseen movement of people strange. Since the audacious, and fatal, passage of the Zeppelin, no lights are allowed, even in windows, after eight. It must have been a terrifying sight in the dark sky. The brightly lighted airship close over the sleeping houses, so light that the number on board could be reckoned. It drifted silently down wind, over the roofs, well inside the defending circle. Then the roar of the propeller began ; the populace rushed out, and there followed a succession of shattering explosions from its ten unseen and ill-directed bombs. Now precautions are taken; and the great silver pencil of the searchlight has swung and passed all to-night over our heads.

No signs of a town besieged.

Prices low, no war feeling, a steady traffic. Only rarely the rattle of an armoured motor through the street; for nearly all military movements are made at night. Except for the universal error of the withholding of news, the control of the population is admirable in its restraint. We have no " nerves " here yet.

Antwerp, Saturday.

The Germans have been forced to keep a retaining army in front of the Belgian lines at Malines. How big this is, it is impossible at present to say. It seems to be no more than a retaining force, protecting communications.

On the other hand, the Belgians have half of their army intact, some 60,000, fresh and in good heart; with the remainder of the troops from Liége, Louvain, and Namur, now reconstituted and keen to keep up their splendid record.

143

FROM THE TRENCHES

It will take an army of 150,000 to invest Antwerp, with its double line of forts.

There is a vague rumour that a secondary and larger force is advancing directly upon Antwerp from the east, independent of the force already facing Malines on the south, and that the big siege guns are being brought up. The eventuality must be contemplated. The Landsturm (reserve army) is already at Liége. The Germans have the reserves to spare, and it would be consistent with their plan to follow their swift-moving columns at the front with a second supporting army, to occupy the conquered territory, already almost evacuated by the advanced troops, and invest Antwerp. If the troops can be spared from Prussia and France, the effort will be made. But not, I think, until the blow at France has failed.

The importance of Antwerp, as the final seat of the Belgian Government and the last base from which the army can operate, cannot be overrated. With Antwerp lost, the army, and all the possibilities of its position upon the German flank, threatening the communications, would be baseless; and must be forced to surrender, or to cut its way through to Ostend.

Germany will mask Antwerp for the present. And later on a siege of Antwerp may not be calculated in terms of Liége. There the Germans attacked with infantry and light field-guns. They have now brought up their heavy siege guns. The rapid fall of the forts of Namur is the measure of the difference.

The outer line of Antwerp forts are one and a half miles apart, alternating fort and redoubt. The silencing of one fort by the heavy guns would leave a gap of three miles, through which troops could be poured.

The Belgian Field Army would have to hold the gap or gaps; behind them the second line of forts would repeat the resistance, in their turn, under increased difficulties. It might cost a number of lives, but of these the Germans are careless. A big army with siege guns could manage it, and not take unduly long.

It will be seen that it is of the utmost importance to protect Antwerp, not by strengthening the defence more than has already been done, but by the operations of a relieving force, acting from the coast, upon the left of the German investing army.

The presence of British troops and ships at Ostend, which has been announced officially in all the Belgian and French papers, has already begun to effect its purpose; by reassuring the Belgians, and distracting the Germans from pouring all their reinforcements on to the front in France.

It is also forcing the light, skirmishing German parties of advance, which threatened the extreme left of the Allied armies, from Courtrai to Dunkirk, to contract.

(The anticipations here outlined have since been borne out closely by the actual events of the fall of Antwerp.)

Sunday.

The Germans resumed their bombardment of Malines yesterday. The church tower provided their chief object. They were successfully kept out of the town.

The news is confirmed that something like a " whole army corps " has been diverted from its advance across the frontier by the spirited sally of the Belgians.

I was down on the lines west of the city again to-day. The troops are in fine spirits at their success. The British sympathy and admiration have been greatly appreciated. The tribute of the House of Commons is spread by the journals broadcast, in large print.

At my small point of view there was only some slight skirmishing. Since four o'clock yesterday the big guns have been having a rest. Some peasants, captured and released, report the retirement of German cavalry upon Louvain. These peasants have had seven days of terror. They, including some women, have been driven at the head of a small German contingent to and fro, threatened with death behind and in front. They relate that those who fell out were shot. Some of them were allowed to stop last night on the steps of the Cathedral, as they were being herded through deserted Malines. They must have been the same whom we saw pass, and heard afterwards murmuring there, while we waited concealed inside.

FROM THE TRENCHES

The large number of Belgian wounds are in the legs; possibly from lying behind two little elevated screens, in place of entrenching; but the German rifle-fire is still low.

The Germans, advancing *en masse*, are constantly described as firing from the hip. In front of the trench which I visited, the ground was cut up by rifle-bullets in a continuous line, a few feet short of the raised bank. Towards the end of the hour I spent there, came a sudden ten minutes of furious firing. The hail of bullets whipped against the far side bank in travelling waves of rustling sound, like the passing of sharp gusts over a moor.

Later.

The air is yellow and heavy from the continuous bombardment of the past days. Sudden showers of rain, out of cloudless skies, come from the same cause. The guns began again to-night.

Ostend, Monday.

The Belgian Army was active this morning. Already at dawn as I passed out of Antwerp through the wire entanglements and small inundations about the military camps, they were on the move for another attack. The guns were in action to the south of us.

The country, in the line of Ghent, is now free. It was possible to travel almost to the French frontier before the alarm of Uhlans began. But the villages, populous and filled with panic last week, are now half deserted and melancholy. The refugees pour aimlessly to the coast and back again, according to the rumours. The railways run, advancing and retreating, according to the movements of the enemy. In the morning trains may run straight, in the evening make a cautious loop. A curious situation, significant of the double occupation of the "open" territory.

I wished to clear up some of the mystery enveloping the northern end of the French frontier. I therefore passed through Ghent westward. Last week I left a German cavalry column disappearing into the silence of "no official news" into the neighbourhood of Courtrai. This afternoon I met news of them, or their like, returning in the same quarter, as I made a hurried run to the border. It was near Yprés that the peasants met us with warnings "The Germans have been sighted, and are expected here."

From a safe retreat, in a wood on rising ground, we watched a small line of German wagons, probably of wounded, winding into and out at the other end of the short village street. It was accompanied and followed by cavalry and a few cars.

It has been heartening to see any Germans facing in the right direction, before I descended once again upon Ostend.

CHAPTER VIII

PARIS AND THE TRENCHES

THE ten days of the great conflict across France were now ended. The military machine, the most powerful that the world has seen, had swept past us across the silence of the frontier. Perfectly prepared beyond all anticipation, and driven by the utmost forces of military despotic tradition, it had achieved a performance remarkable in the history of wars. But the machine had been met, and though we did not yet know it, the momentum of its hammer-blow had been exhausted, by a defensive retreat which will rank as unsurpassed not only in military history but in the record of the greatest feats of human endurance, of the supreme conquests of the spirit of man over the machinery of man's invention.

Outmatched by ten to one, fighting by regiments, by groups, by individuals, the soldiers of the independent racial spirit, of voluntary subordination to the service of war, had resisted, doggedly, inch by inch, and outlasted in the end, the devastating impetus of the vast war engine. Still an unbeaten army of unconquerable personality, the survivors waited outside Paris, reinforced, ready to resume the offensive. Failure in organisation, suspected failures in collaboration might have been fatal to the moral of a mechanically trained army. To the elastic temperament and combination of our soldiers, bringing each a free man's personality to the work of his chosen profession, nothing could be fatal but loss of life itself, or loss of faith in the common cause.

I returned again to Paris when the Germans were within a long march of the outer forts. The journey took an interminable time. The direct lines were threatened by the enemy or blocked with the movements of troops. We wandered to remote junctions west of Paris, and had to fight good-humouredly for standing-room with crowds of reservists recalled to the colours. No doubt owing to the greater magnitude of the problem the French railway organisation, for other than military service, did not compare well, during the earlier stages of the war, with that of the Belgians, who showed a remarkable power of keeping their ordinary traffic almost normal, and of reconciling it with the movements of their own or the enemy's troops.

Paris was practically empty. A second greater exodus was going on. The Government had retired to Bordeaux the day before. With few exceptions even the war correspondents, the last usually to cling on, had vanished. Our Embassy had left with the Government. Our Consulate had also vanished, leaving a large number of anxious countrymen stranded. Doubtless they acted under orders. But, in pleasing contrast, a few of our Consuls seem to have been allowed to exercise a more considerate discretion, and remained doing excellent service till the threat of occupation passed. Most of the Government offices were being occupied by soldiers. General Gallieni, the Military Governor, was taking a firm hold. We felt at once that the defence of Paris in his hands was to be really " *jusqu'au bout.*"

Life in Paris was undergoing a second mutation. On the occasion of my first visit, at the outbreak of the war, it was in the throes attending the surrender of individual liberty to the control of the Departments of official military government. The Departments had now retreated, and civilian life was under the necessity of readjusting itself to the confused beginnings of a purely " soldier " rule. The inconveniences lasted only for a few days. The Military Governor organised his staff for the unaccustomed work of administration with conspicuous energy.

All that was left of Paris, passive, observant, and quick to grasp the necessity of subduing even its natural inclination to caustic comment, accepted the situation philosophically. For a day or two we still listened for the sound of the guns of the forts, which should announce the beginning of the siege. But in place of them came the quick rumour of the British successes near Compiègne, of the German faltering and hesitation, of the swing south, and finally of the retreat from the Marne. People began to return. Paris life regained something of its vivacity; only the dark quiet evenings, and the occasional visit of an airman, survived inside the defences to remind us of the war. Now and then the sight of a British soldier being embraced on the streets, and treated to an extent that jeopardised the influence of Lord Kitchener's letter, made a link with the withdrawing armies. News was reduced to the customary minimum.

In the trenches, Friday.

Here, outside the gates of Paris, within the circle of the forts, there is a note of instancy and reality which is hardly shared by the city itself even since the nearer approach of the invaders. The red and blue dots of soldiers move briskly with purpose over the fields, under the heavy, summer trees. Just a flash of sun here and there on bayonet or helmet.

Fortune has introduced me to a collection of non-commissioned officers—jolly fellows, in good heart. Some spoke English. One was a Russian who had served as a volunteer in most of the armies of the world. We sat under a tree in the shade, and they superintended the heavy work of more red dots with grey shirts, sweltering in the sun and digging trenches in the dusty, brown soil. In the distance, business-like little lines of blue and red moved away over the horizon. For the German cavalry is near us, in the Forest of Compiégne, to the north. It had reached to Soissons, even to Creil, yesterday.

The British caught them well two days ago; but now they are between us and the British, in their distracting, scattered Uhlan fashion.

We do not ask now: " Where are the English ? " We know ! But now it is : " Where are the Indian troops ? How many are they ? Where do they land ? " Most of my friends are volunteers, full of spirit, and new to the work. We are rather puzzled by the position. Of course the German strategy is contrary to all sound rule. But still the " strategic retreat " seems to have drawn out the French lines almost as long as the line to the German base. We appear to pin our faith to that mysterious unknown factor, of which the Press speaks, and to the Indians and Turcos, and other oddments.

Then comes the interruption of reality. A few dispatch riders, in faint dusty blue, gallop past. A few wounded, supported, bandaged, or carried, come more slowly through the hot fields, along the dusty trenches and entanglements. A German mitrailleuse car, "blindée" (armoured)—that French invention that the Germans have turned to such account—has rushed on a French outpost. These are its victims. But the car is—we are told—" accounted for."

The touch of war is only a momentary disturbance to the quiet, busy work of the red-and-blue and red-and-grey dots, marching and mattocking in the afternoon sun round us.

Paris itself is "empty." Four weeks ago the Boulevards were deserted, but it was the emptiness of emotional stress, varied by the rush of sudden crowds and alarms. This was followed by our declaration of war; and coincidentally the streets grew again alive. Now they are deserted, but this time in earnest, for the inhabitants have dispersed where they may. There s no panic; none of the " nerves " of a month ago. The little unrest is due to the *reductio ad absurdum* of war news, which characterises this war in all countries. The only crowd to-day was the crowd of automobiles at the Invalides, getting permits to leave the city before 7.30 to-night, the last moment of passage permitted. Even the 5 o'clock circuit of German aeroplanes created small sensation. It is no longer "new." Yesterday, gentlemen of sporting tastes took shots at the aeroplanes, as they sat at coffee on the Boulevards. To-day, some of the Brussels caution, which found in such promiscuous shooting a yet greater danger for the inhabitants, has asserted itself. A mitrailleuse on the Madeleine secures the civic safety.

Four weeks ago chance made it necessary for me to pass hours in almost every Government office in the city. There was then the inevitable confusion due to the fact that most of the efficient staff had gone to the front just at the moment at which every individual found his rights to move and exist had become vested in a series of public offices, and no longer in himself. Chance took me to-day to wait in almost all these offices yet once again. It was again a moment of dislocation, for the Government have gone. The offices are in the hands of soldiers. The citizens have to adjust their existence anew to yet another control, that of a purely military organisation.

All the landmarks are shifted. Begins anew the scuffle for the usual permissions to move or exist. As a pleasant contrast to the general flight and upheaval, the United States Embassy and Consulate are looking after the individual anxieties of half the nationalities of Europe with a courtesy and efficiency beyond all praise. Paris is empty, but sunny and still itself. Through the empty street the columns of red and blue soldiers pass, with dusty boots, making bright streaks of colour. Like a mother of pearl shell left on the beach, the colours of Paris remain vivid, though the life in her Government is gone south.

FROM THE TRENCHES

Friday night.

Another interlude — Shakespearean if you like. The talk of the first and second Watchmen and the second Citizen outside the walls. A drop-scene before Paris, in the second act of the great war tragedy.

The gates had closed before I could get in. A corporal, who considered himself under an obligation, suggested taking refuge in a shelter with five non-commissioned officers, who were superintending the defence works. He knew one of them. The rest were not of his regiment, and suspicious, as men are behind the lines. But two or three gathered round to smoke; and, Parisian-like, thawed with their own talk. The rest rolled up on the straw, and moved restlessly in tired sleep, outside the range of the single light.

Naturally the talk turned first on the stranger: " What a risky job. Now, a soldier goes safely where he's told, and can fight there, with friends round. But you may be shot by anyone, as the easiest thing to do! No inquiries as in peace time. Anyone may do it; and it's only

160

an unlucky incident. No mention in the papers even! Why, even generals and officers have been shot in this war by mistake."

The risk set my corporal talking of a younger brother of his, whom he had brought up and seen married; their two wives are together at home with the babies. " He is of the —1st line, the little brother—only so high. I do not know where he is. Only one postcard with no date or address, saying ' Still living.' That is all, two weeks ago; and the war may be over, and we shall never know. Perhaps we shall have his regimental number returned, and never know. The little one whom I brought up—only so high."

There was only one opinion about the English troops. " What fellows they are—*charmants garcons!*—big and cool-looking in their ' green '; and impassive! And then, so gay, always so gay—except their songs!"

" I cannot understand them, but they laugh all the time, even when they are too tired to walk;"—it was a cuirassier speaking—"I helped to carry one in the other day; four of us. It was near Amiens. He was dying; his legs—so. He kept on saying something which we could not understand; perhaps it was a message to his mother or sweetheart. But he smiled always, and shook hands. And he said: ' Good friends. Good old England.' I understood that. He died before we found the ambulance.''

I asked cautiously, later, why there was the constant question about the whereabouts of the " Turcos," Indians and Japanese. Were we not enough ? There was a volume of answer. " Ah, but we are civilised ! We thought this fighting would be civilised. They cut the heads off their bullets. Here is one ! And they rough the edge of their bayonets—I have picked them up ! But it is with savages. And we have not the temperament." A volunteer emphasised this, a bearded manufacturer, with a family, in ordinary times: " And these others know the barbarous methods of fight. It is of their nature. They can be ferocious. The savages fear them.''

The old walls of Paris, the third line of defence, remain a cherished sentiment. The famous story of Todleben riding round them on inspection, with two officers, in silence, and only remarking quietly at the end : " *C'est tout ? Paris est prise d'avance !* " was treated as a German's joke !

" The walls ? They will be fought to the last ! The stones of the street of Paris will rise up in new barricades—if ' they ' get so far ! "

A volunteer infantryman arrived with a packet of salt. Salt is getting rare. The arrival was made the occasion of a quick cooking of the universal soup. The talk flickered up ; chiefly of friends and positions of regiments, details confused and not to be recorded. The end of one story, however, stands out vividly : " We were only three, and he could not walk further, and it was a cold night. We could not put him in a haystack, for the ' Bosches ' burn them ; or in a cottage, till ' they ' had gone past. So we made a shallow trough between the furrows, leaving him warm with his head uncovered, and pulled a harrow above him. In the morning the peasant who had left the harrow would find him, warm ; or it would be easy to finish burying him."

FROM THE TRENCHES

The last of them rolled up in their coats and straw to sleep, my corporal still murmuring : " I wonder where he is, the little one—so high ? Perhaps, after the war—— "

And it seemed only a moment later that the dawn began behind Paris, yellow behind the grey towers above the still mists.

Paris, Saturday dawn.

During the respite of the last days the army of defence has at least got what sleep it could.

The trenches within the circle of forts are cloaked before dawn by mist. Here and there, hidden under temporary shelters, a groan or murmur tells where the soldiers sleep on straw, behind the entrenchments. The stations of the local railway lines are filled with straw, and among sacks and accoutrements the more fortunate are asleep, crowded close under the open sheds.

If I move my head, shadows loom out of the mist—the close-standing sentries. Singular figures, hidden in white vapour to the waist.

164

PARIS AND THE TRENCHES

All wearing heavy cloaks of different types, but made uniform by the military cap, the shouldered or grounded musket.

The challenges run round, in subdued tones. Even suspicion seems lulled. In the truce of the night the mind even of the sentry is passive. The artificial atmosphere, that makes all but the known uniform an enemy, is forgotten for the moment.

Back towards Paris, the city is shoulder-deep in white mist. Only the spires and towers emerge, grey and sleepy. The summit of the Eiffel Tower is lost again in a yet higher belt.

As the grey light grows yellow and red with the coming sun, the towers are projected against it as if floating in mid air, a city of dreams. Can this be the town that is waiting half empty, garrisoned with soldiers, every public office a barrack or ambulance, for expected bombardment, almost certain siege ?

Yet only a few miles to the north—how few the citizens do not yet know—the advance patrols of the enemy are also resting, sleeping under the same bands of white mist. They are at Pontoise; some of them have been encountered even near the Seine in the glades of the Forest of St. Germain.

And behind us, also hidden by the mist, the restless movement of our own troops continues. Trains are shunting and banging; there is the rattle of heavy wheels on the roads. . . .

The yellow light widens; the mist lifts and grows thin. The sentries seem to shape themselves, and swing their cloaks. A general stir rustles out of the shelters. The clatter of cooking-pots and boots, even of voices, begins round us. The night has been warm, and a sultry feeling falls again at once with the opening of day. A cavalry patrol, visible already in its lighter blue uniforms, files past. The men move out to their work on the earthworks. There is the rattle of arms as the rifles are freed from their standing stooks. Strange sheaves these, in their threatening lines, by the edges of uncut cornfields. They begin to glitter as they are lifted in the early sunlight.

The sound of a distant shot, unexplained, startles my little circle of view into alertness.

PARIS AND THE TRENCHES

The truce of night goes in an instant with the mist. Suspicion, the sharp tension of prospective attack, change in a second the atmosphere. Orders, loud voices, and movements tell the beginning of another inconsequent day in the unnatural war.

Paris, as I return, is already awake: sharp outlined and stirring. Carts are moving in and out of one gate, which has opened early. Small parties of officers roll out noisily in motor-cars from their city quarters.

It is time to get back to the suppressed, shepherded existence of a civilian in a town under military government, for whom rumour-fed ignorance is considered to be the only safe-guard against panic.

Psychology of an elementary character might form a part of the training of the experts in war.

Paris, Saturday midnight.

The pause outside Paris continues. It is neither ominous nor reassuring. After their astonishing march the Germans have to collect

167

themselves for the great move. Rushed by their pace and volume, but acting on a concerted plan, the Allies have retired with deliberate skill upon their intended positions; with Paris as pivot. For the time fighting tactics are of less importance. Strategy, for the first time since the failure beyond the frontier, is again to decide.

The Germans have failed to force a decisive victory on their course across France. The Allied Armies are still unseparated, their temporary dislocation is cemented five times as strongly. Havre is still covered, Paris is covered, the connection is retained with the armies in Lorraine. The Crown Prince's army has failed to keep pace in the centre. The front for the Allies is contracted; they have again a strategic base on Paris; they have succeeded in gaining, in spite of the tremendous pursuit, their chosen lines of defence to north and east of the capital.

During the last few days the Germans have discovered the strength of the position of the Allies by means of their unsuccessful raids at Compiègne and elsewhere. They have possibly got some further news from the west. They have had to rest their men and horses after the terrific march; get up their great siege guns; prepare their positions and platforms, and reconnoitre the admirable defensive strategic positions. Do they mean to attack Paris? There is now doubt of it. It has been "Paris or die." May we hope the "die" will be cast?

There has been a considerable movement of their troops to the south, east of Saint Denis. This has been construed into an attempt to turn the rear of the French positions on the frontier; to create a diversion in favour of the Crown Prince's army; to link up with this, and either surround the French army of Lorraine or advance in double force on Paris. This would imply a hesitation in the advance of the terrible "marching column," a relenting of the pace—in fact, a blunder of magnitude, in view of the importance of time.

It is more than probable that the movement south, to the east of Paris, is preparatory to an advance upon the capital from two directions, the east and north-east. This would at once threaten the connection with the armies of

FROM THE TRENCHES

Lorraine; do something to clear the road for the Crown Prince in the centre; and substitute for an immediate attack upon Paris an advance upon the main position of our armies.

The design is being retarded by the usual measures; measures which, to the lay mind, might well have been employed in retarding the advance through Flanders and mid-Belgium.

Paris is going to be defended to the last wall. General Gallieni's thirty-eight-word proclamation has created a profound impression. If it comes even to street fighting, the few survivors in the city here are prepared to see the walls burning about them.

Perhaps I may mention the open secret that, if the Germans are rejoicing in the progress of their great siege guns, towed by 30-50 horses, we have a surprise quite as cheering for them here, once they get to close grips.

And besides this, we are all asking ourselves how long their nice sense of humanity will prevent the French making more use of their explosive secret? This is a war to kill, to be decided by the number killed.

PARIS AND THE TRENCHES

And then Lord Kitchener's " unknown factor " ;
we know a great deal about it now.

General Gallieni is an administrator of established reputation, and a fighter by temperament.
I met him to-day on his round of the fortifications.
He is never away from the vital points ; at the
same time his administration of the town has got
into working order with rapidity. He passed,
with a salute, in a cloud of dust, the car in front
guarded by a black orderly.

And even if Paris goes ? Well, the campaign
is clear. Sentiment is not to interfere with this
ingenious campaign against superior forces.

It is impatient work, waiting in a placid town
for an unheard enemy. I went out to look for
him to-day. The roving " Uhlan," the " hooli-
gan " of the war, had been reported yesterday at
Pontoise, and in the Forest of St. Germain. I
had an enchanting tour through the long glades,
in sunlight, for my pains. Not the gleam
of a lance as far even as Pontoise. The windings of the Seine were only alive with boys
bathing and the sharp detail of red and blue
sentries on the bridges. Many bridges are closed,

but there is none of the worry of the stops by
" Civic Guards " at every corner that jolted one
in Belgium. The challenges are rare, and
business-like.

I ran all through the forest, cheated of even
a " view " of the enemy. It is not saying much
to say that our lines are not yet back upon the
Seine. The French aviators floated overhead,
but not even the audacious " Taube " broke the
blue and green of sky and forest.

At Versailles I ran again into the suspicious
atmosphere of the purely military town. Hardly
a civilian to be seen. All houses closed. Why
is the purely military town the most nervous ?
At Paris we look calmly even on aviators and
dragoons; only the British soldier, one of the
many " missing " returning now in numbers to
rejoin their units via Paris, is overwhelmed with
greetings, little crowds, and embraces. But at
Versailles the vibration of war nerves made
every bare cobbled street " jumpy " in atmosphere.

All along the shady roads through the forests
of Marly wound the peasant carts, freighted with

refugee women and children. Under the trees
by the wayside carts in hundreds were drawn up,
loaded with household goods and trusses of hay
or straw for the patient horse or donkey. The
women sat round cooking-pots set on wood fires.
The children played noisily. The chief game
was " Germans "—a tin pot on a stone, at which a
gipsy-looking band hurled bricks from a safe ten
feet.

Drifting aimlessly here and there, ready to
move at a rumour, the great army of the homeless, just as in Belgium, moves through the
fertile fields. It is depressed, purposeless,
puzzled. Turned back from the big towns, re-
luctant to cross the Channel, uprooted from the
home-fields, like plants torn up and swirled endlessly in a weir pool—moving endlessly back and
forwards. The generations of peace, the rich
product of human progress, that war is killing.

Through their unheeding lines on either side
passed ceaselessly the wagon-loads of hay, the
munition carts, the cavalry patrols, all the
sacrifices to the new idol of devastation. We
are long past cheering soldiers in the war-lands.

CHAPTER IX

The Movements in the North

Sunday night.

THE Germans are turning sharply south, descending diagonally on the east of Paris. The country they held, or partially held, three days ago, as far west as Compiègne, Gisors, and Pontoise, is now free of all but isolated patrols. The brilliant cavalry action at Compiègne, where the British lost six and recovered sixteen guns, may have been but a feint to cover the alteration of direction. Amiens they still hold, and the line due south of it. Our forces, keeping touch with the enemy, have moved forward their covering line across and to the east of Paris on the side of the Marne, with a curve south near Paris on their left wing. What is the reason of the change? Is it merely a move in the great chess game designed at Berlin; first the powerful

174

"marching column" striking directly at the more vulnerable north-west corner of Paris, so as to draw out the French defence in that direction, thinning its connecting links with the eastern army; then a swift change, and a blow at the weakened centre, with the intention of cutting off and surrounding the eastern army very near to fatal Sedan?

Is it an attempt to force a decisive action before attacking Paris, since the Allies, in spite of their costly retreat, are still an undefeated army, now safely established in a strong defensive position? Is it this attempt, combined with the intention of joining forces with the Rheims armies of von Buelow and Wurtemberg, and of cutting communications behind the army opposing the Crown Prince?

Or has there really been some definite change of plan forced upon the northern army of von Kluck? Has he recognised the danger of pressing in upon Paris from the north and north-west between the scissors of the armies in the Marne and of some other army in the west and north, still unknown to us. The difficult change of line

175

s, in that case, to be made in order to secure a concentration of the armies, and a later attack on Paris from the east. This I suggested as an explanation yesterday. It is the more certain coup, if it can be brought off; and it is less exposed during its operation to any threat from the north than would be a diagonal blow at north-west Paris. A few days will show; but I expect to hear shortly that the armies have been engaged on the east side of the Oise, along the Marne.

I traversed to-day all the region from Paris to the north country, passing through the subtle Paris entrenchments and over the nervous Seine bridges, all ready to be dynamited.

The country, forest and field, was strikingly beautiful in really hot sunshine. But empty. The picturesque white villages were deserted and green-shuttered; the grey stone towns with only a few silent soft-footed peasants, and solitary neglected children. Here and there a few black-hooded women were hanging a wayside cross or shrine with votive flowers. There was again the oppressive expectant feeling of the country that is left open to the enemy, undefended. Under the trees, or trekking aimlessly along the roads, knots and processions of homeless peasants, with their high carts heaped with household goods. Here and there a little drove of their cattle. All the folk, brown, depressed but resigned. As the tide of Germans has passed south and east, they have been creeping inevitably back, with a sort of homing instinct. A few blue cavalry patrols, French, caused them succeeding fear and reassurance. Magny, Mantes, Gisors, Gournay, Beauvais, back and fro, we made certain that the tide was retreating; and followed on the tail of our own advance close enough to get clear as to the general position. The wayside refugees were from local villages, and we could do little to relieve them except to help some of the more helpless on their way.

At Pontoise, a French cavalry column was passing through eastward, the direction of the new move. The women stood ready with bottles and jugs, and ran beside the horses to receive back the glasses, cramming cigarettes into the smiling troopers' hands. Several of the men, with difficulty controlling their horses, plucked the red wool tassels from their epaulettes, and gave them in return as souvenirs.

At Mantes we came upon a collection of motors, families flying from Paris to the north on the safe western route. For miles together we ran through entrenchments and fortified positions, prepared to meet the expected stroke of the hammer at the west of Paris. Only a few troops remained in the trenches, sparks of colour through the orchards on the great rolling wooded uplands. The others have moved eastwards, to the scene of the battle now imminent on the east of Paris.

We met a brown, battered company of our own men also. They were resting from their exhausting retreat, and lined the roads, cheerfully greeting columns of French who moved eastward past and through them.

Later, the shuttle was weaving in different fashion. Here, on road and train, our troops in their turn—but this time fresh-complexioned reinforcements—were pouring eastward; while the worn-looking French soldiers stood aside, or lay resting to let them pass, with hearty jokes and salutes.

Then we ran out north into open undefended territory. Again deserted villages. Now and then a sharp contrast, when we hit some level crossing, and a line of trains passed us, pouring continually south with crowded carriages and trucks of ever fresh reinforcements.

Beauvais is unoccupied by either side, but it remains a funereal town. A few women in black, a few inhabitants creeping back. Silent clusters on the Cathedral steps.

Here an incident occurred, illustrative of the interpenetration of the armies in these " open " districts.

We were sitting at coffee in the square. A car, blowing a continuous blast, rushed through. In it were two grey figures, German officers, with a grey-tunicked driver. They flashed through, sitting very low. Immediately there was a quick, quiet rush of women and boys to the shelter of the Mairie and the Cathedral. The movement seemed instinctive. Their faces remained expressionless, almost apathetic.

FROM THE TRENCHES

Ten minutes later we were carefully leaving the town. When the German patrols take to motors, one cannot count upon the start we had in Belgium against the customary Uhlan horse. Another motor dashed quickly past. In it were two other grey-tunicked German cavalrymen. But these were prisoners, being run through south from near Amiens. Supposing these two cars had met, what would have happened ?

I have asked a number of questions, to some of which we know the answers. I will venture one more. Why have the valuable little sea-ports been left absolutely unguarded against the small raiding German patrols that alone at present threaten all the coast ? Not an army of occupation, but a few hardened men landed, would be sufficient to protect much that is valuable, but which now lies open to any chance three men with arms. And time allows the Germans to spare little more.

Monday.

The great battle on the new front has begun. This is the third day of the fighting. The

THE MOVEMENTS IN THE NORTH

German left, pushing south past Ourcq, got as far as Coulommiers, at the same time pressing upon Paris from the east. They have retired again upon Meaux, in this quarter. Of the fortunes further east there is no news. The British troops are holding a vital point in the defensive against the double move, the direct blow south and the eastern attack upon the city.

The countermove of the Allied left wing to meet the German change of front has been carried out with remarkable rapidity. The alternate passing of our own and the French troops through each other's positions in taking up their fresh lines was an interesting time of intricate manœuvre to watch. Paris has become a pivot; no longer the direct object of defence or attack. Any victory of the German right outside the eastern line of defence, would have the advantage for the Germans of sending both armies intermingled back upon and through the forts, impeding their fire. The new move thus places Paris in the position of the prize of the battle.

FROM THE TRENCHES

The north is clear of both armies. Amiens is the most westerly town occupied by the enemy. The new position of the Allies has led to an abandonment of all the seaports. The inhabitants have been ordered to disarm, and the bases and stores have been removed.

The recent moves of the Allies have suggested, in their mass, remarkable mobility and promptitude. They have worked with a precision and simplicity that have made them seem the product of very cool design, and even of long anticipation. The Germans would seem to have made the mistake of considering our army out of the game. They have advanced heedlessly across it, unaware of its elastic recovery and of its reinforcement.

The very complexity of the few moves met with in detail during the last few days has given considerable reassurance. Their very disconnection from the course of apparent events, engagements already officially acknowledged, shows them to be no expedient of the moment, but part of a prepared scheme, played now on

182

the chosen field, and with the moves following an expected order.

I have been spending most of the day witnessing the development of one of the expected moves. The sunlit fields were alive with marching troops. The headquarters, at Rouen, were crowded with staff officers. Several nationalities and all arms were represented. There was the quivering suspicious atmosphere that accompanies an action in near prospect. Beyond certain boundaries, Evreux, Les Andelys, Gisors, I was told I should go in " peril of life," "at my own risk." Long before I had traversed them sufficiently to be satisfied of the positions, through the orderly, coloured confusion of an army in the field, the risk had been sufficient, without crossing the bounds to find the enemy. There was anxiety, strain, but there was the new excitement of men on the offensive. We are assured of our defensive lines. We can afford to take the initiative.

There was plenty of personal incident—a conversation with a fierce general in a shady, deserted château, agreeable in process and issue ;

arrest and escort by a clattering Lancer patrol; the sight of dismounted cavalrymen making embrasures in the walls of an orchard, with momentarily turned, scowling faces.

In general purport the hours with this elusive force were more interesting than the sight of an actual engagement—that is, all the spectator can see of one.

Later in the day, in the course of a wide circle, I came down from the north on the rear of the German right flank. This country was supposed to be deserted. But the German army is well in touch with the chess-board in the north and west. The peasants told me of the proximity of two hundred Uhlans and a battery of guns. But it was impossible to find any trace of a further German advance westward.

The check to the Germans near Coulommiers is promising. Their right wing seems to have recognised that the forces opposed are too strong, for several reasons, for their congenial fashion of attack, and is falling back. Their combined armies have withdrawn too far south-east to attack Paris again by any surprise move.

THE MOVEMENTS IN THE NORTH

They have been moving to break the line of our armies opposed to them directly south, and to cut through them well east of Paris, towards Sézanne. There is a general atmosphere of reassurance among our troops to-day. The tide has turned, and I date the turn from *September 6th.*

Tuesday.

There is a very satisfactory development of the position beginning on the west of Paris. Much of the north-west region, which for a time was left unoccupied (including the sea-ports), is again in process of resumption. The rapidity of the German hammer-attack made a concentration of our troops necessary outside the weaker defences of the city. It was remarkable the pace and precision with which the Allied armies, after ten days of continuous fighting, and their hurry of difficult retreat across France, took up position on their new base at Paris. They converted a widespread movement of detensive retreat, over an infinite number of small tactical points, into a finely consolidated, new strategic position. But they could do no

185

more for the moment in the north than hold the railway lines through which the reinforcements were being poured.

Then came the German new front to the south. The Allies' reinforcements had to swing to meet them, or rather to pour men across to adjust the balance at the threatened points. To this the fresh British reinforcements were specially devoted; again to hold the key, and more than one key, of the new lines of defence.

The movement is complete. Strengthened at the weak link, the French have been able again to set their grasp upon the " open " country of the line north of the Seine. The boundaries of the extension, and the ultimate intention of the movement may be best left to the intelligent to surmise. Its significance for us is its re-assurance as to the confidence of our armies in the strength of their eastern line of defence, its evidence that they are now strong enough to attempt in turn offensive movements and resume their connections, only briefly threatened and never entirely interrupted, with their north-western sea-bases.

THE MOVEMENTS IN THE NORTH

The last two days have been spent in following this movement in far more detail than can yet be written. Its interest has been due to its moral effect as much as to its strategical importance. The great issue is being fought out, for the present, on the east of Paris.

After leaving our new headquarters to-day we swung across to the east. The country—Forges, Gournay, Gisors, Clermont—is still unoccupied. The beautiful brown and grey stone villages with faint-red roofs and dark mediæval gateways are shuttered and empty. A few noiseless children, a woman or two, a hungry couple of curs on the dusty cobbles. The roads are clear of refugees, wandered further afield in their high-wheeled laden carts. Only here and there a few stolid, hardy or resigned village folk cling on, and form clusters before a solitary open restaurant, headed by some sturdy Maire. The restaurant has still good bread and wine, nothing more.

The fields are almost deserted; miles of rich meadow and crops in the white sunshine. One or two farmers or women with stout little sons at work in the crops, make rare and startling breaks in the passing lonely landscape.

But there was a change to-day. Every now and then in remote places a scouting car with a splash of uniforms, or a vicious-looking mitrailleuse car with helmets cloaked in linen, threatening over its grey edges, met us in the miles of shaded lanes.

Some of the small towns had again guards, military or civic, who gave us pause; while each protested that the new military control had made some different kind of " pass " necessary. Some wanted a red one, some a blue. Some wanted a " visé " from the local Maire. Fortunately during most of the hot day the Maires were absent or asleep, and it was agreed to be better to wake the one at the next village. The next village was generally also asserted to be a regimental headquarters. In these cases it usually proved to be utterly deserted.

In one little town, near Clermont, we came in for a strange echo of the war. A woman in a high cart drove past quickly, while we were talking with the Maire and the woman of the inn. There was a sudden silence, Then a dramatic, passionate outburst from the handsome, sibyl-faced hostess, who had two sons at the war :

" Think of it : that woman ! There were three of our soldiers chased from the fight at Creil. They took refuge with her. She is rich and has a garden. She hid them in the hayloft; threw their uniforms in the garden. The Germans came. They slept in her house. They said : ' We are forced to fight; it is not of our seeking : the French attacked us.' They found the uniforms. They put a pistol to her breast : ' We will shoot you if you do not say where are those soldiers.' She cried : " In the loft." They shot them ; all three. The traitress !—and it would have been so easy for a woman to lie ! "

A village near Creil itself gave us another echo. A German field-cap hung over the forge. The old smith, one of the last men now left in the village, explained it had fallen from the head of one of three or four German soldiers who had been chased through the street a few days before.

FROM THE TRENCHES

"It shall hang there till the owner returns for it," he added grimly, "May my great-grand-children see it still hanging so!"

And yet one more, and this within sound of the guns, that have been echoing nearer or fainter these last days. A woman ran out of the door of a solitary cottage towards Senlis, waving her arm. One stops quickly these days. A man was dying inside. She had burned his uniform; but I knew at once he was a German. He had been shot while scouting; had hid himself, and crawled to her house. We did what we could for him. From him I learned that the Germans are already reinforcing to meet the western move, and of many things that are hidden from us—no doubt, for our good— or vaguely guessed at. It was no matter of "communication with the enemy"; he was already past the line that divides small irritable tribal mortals; he was joining issue with the last great common foe.

We left him to die in the care of the woman who had not "passed by on the other side." Her son would visit her shortly—she had refused to leave her cottage—and would bury him in the field. No one else was to know.

This is the meaning of the machine of war: The man joins the machine for the honour of the nation. The machine drives him, one of a nameless herd, for a few days, beyond his strength, to his death, for the honour of the machine. And yet the nation is made up of the men; and the machine is made up of the men; and the men die. But for such machines we should know better what is the honour of the nation—that is, of the men—for the men would judge of it, as men, for themselves.

We approached as near as we could venture— for we were behind the enemy—north of Betz and close to the sound of the guns. We saw as much as anyone is likely to see of the fighting in such warfare: the distant sight of greeny-white smoke-balls bursting over trees on a far hill; the slight movement, round the edges of distant woods that sloped towards us, of small grey dots, that were assumed to be the enemy.

Returning across the north of Paris by circuitous ways, we came round by the west, through the entrenched positions. During the day we passed over five bridges already mined with dynamite, and one wooden bridge with the props half cut through. It is a stimulating experience to crawl over bridges, like Kew Bridge for size and sunny situation, with the warning from armed soldiers at either end that too much vibration may send them exploding into the air, or dropping into the river. We are warned to avoid even the comfort of a cigarette; and there are other impediments to make the passage tortuous and exciting.

The one relief on nearing Paris is the infection of its unconquerable gaiety. After days in the terrible " war atmosphere," every face suspicious, every mile a wrestle with the shadow of puzzled mistrust, it was a lightening of the whole evening when two veteran " grey moustaches " levelled their muskets on a bridge, and threatened to shoot us with a twinkle in their blue eyes—the first smile of the day.

And this is only one day on the fringe of the great struggle of whose incident, triumph, and lonely death there shall be small record.

CHAPTER X

THE BATTLES ON THE MARNE

TUESDAY'S distant sight of the Germans moving
north-west across the hills above Betz was in
reality a side-view of the masterly and rapid
retreat that von Kluck made from the Battles
on the Marne. The French and our own troops
were close on his heels; but so skilfully was the
retreat executed that our cavalry was unable
to operate effectively, and the German western
armies extricated themselves from our enveloping movement without severe defeat. They
were falling back at express speed upon the
position already selected along the heights
behind the Aisne. On the morning after regaining Paris I ran out through Lagny to Meaux, to
follow up the line of the battles.

Paris, Thursday.

Those have been grim fights round Meaux

the last few days. It is no single battlefield; rather a continuous line of battles. But Chaucotin, Poincy, Penchard, Chambery, may be remembered in history as the triangle where the flood was first turned back. The line is marked on the fields like the waving edge of a past tide on the beach—those pleasant fields, stubble, meadow, trees, that fall from either side to the wooded, sheltered river; and among them, caught as in a hollow, Meaux itself, its cathedral, by some miracle, still unharmed.

The loss has been great, especially on the side of the Germans. The peasants to-day were shovelling into the long trenches the terrible harvest of death. All round us was the litter of battle, smashed muskets, smashed helmets, and broken life.

I could follow the fighting foot by foot from well south of Meaux. Haystacks torn down and scattered over the field for trusses of shelter. Haystacks still standing, their north side torn and holed with shrapnel, with trusses like wings on either side whence the men had fired. Burnt woods, trees cut down and broken, and the long brown lines of trenches.

Some of our own men took me round them. Trenches finely made but, in the hurry, not so finished as those which the Italian workmen, turned on to this surprising task instead of digging the Metropolitan tunnels, have made near Paris.

The German trenches were distinguishable by their shape, more hurried, as of the attacking side. It was possible to follow the story—the trenches where the shell had burst well behind; the tell-tale breaks where the Germans had found the range; the trample and dead horses of cavalry charges.

At Penchard our —— division had suffered fearfully. Before they fired a shot the Germans had the range; and the men stood by helplessly or ran back—those who survived. But the Germans are far on the retreat now from Penchard!

At Poincy they played yet another trick, and paid for it. Beaten by our close fire from the trenches—how close I could measure—one in every three Germans got up and ran back, leaving two or three hidden. Our men came quickly up, taking no cover. From close range they were swept away by the unexpected fire. But they came back—with the bayonet! " And, sir, the Prussians don't like cold steel. But we left them no time to say so ! "

At Chaucotin the peasants were burying many hundred Germans, by the trenches, in a wastage of swords, muskets, and broken saddles and arms. And in the distance, beyond the Marne and Ourcq, the battle we could hear still going on.

In Meaux, as I looked over the bridge, the steam-barges deep in the green shadow of the river below were moving slowly towards Paris with yet more wounded. The decks were bright with the blue-red guards.

Even on this side of Meaux overturned wagons, sunken barges, and the inevitable trenches and piled trusses told of some hours of the day-long battles. Further forward, on the Ourcq, were torn and scrambled banks, where, I was told, our cavalry drove the enemy actually into the canal. Our cavalry has done magnificently.

It was jolly in Meaux to hear good northern English, and English with a brogue, and to see the confident, bronzed faces. The men are in great heart. " I have had five weeks out of bed. It's a bit slow here "—this town was all but deserted—" but it's a lark. We've got 'em ! "

Man to man, and against odds, on these fields the British and French have flung back the weight of the tide.

Beyond Chambery there was yet another sign —a collection of 150 German wounded, waiting to be brought down. At last we were following an advance, if only in a small corner of the great field.

Through all the villages along the Marne those who loitered by the silent closed houses showed holiday faces. Close outside Paris life seemed to be hardly affected. It came as a surprise, in the sunny fields, to pass by long, noisy trains of motor-lorries, bearing an infinite number of names of firms. And longer, slower trains of wagons with white and dappled grey horses were dragging in captured German pontoons, splashed with coloured soldiers. Some of these were even sitting in rope-nooses slung from the projecting beams. About them, the files of tramping infantry or fretting cavalry.

One of these motor-wagons to-day saved us a shock, and gave us a spectacle. Taking a wrong turn, which we followed, it ran down a steep road to Esbly, and, just ahead of us, shot over the edge of an exploded bridge into the river. The driver got out by jumping in time. The village was quite deserted.

In war time there are only a few through routes left open. The rest are torn up or blocked. Every exit from a town, except one or two, is barricaded with piles of trees, stone-sacks, logs, hoardings, wire, and earth. In some cases the loose structures threaten more danger to the defenders. The through routes left are broken up at intervals by walls and pits, mazes through which one winds precariously. The barricades are held by stern soldiers. But the army of Paris has admirable manners.

Probably few civilians in this war will be able

to see the " Military Zone " of Paris. Yet it is a wonderful sight. Twice I ran through it to-day. Vast grounds, with horses exercising, ridden by grey soldiers. Huge parks of guns, guarded by blue soldiers. Immense enclosures of cattle. Lines of stacks; stores of forage of all sorts; acres of wagons; sprinkled with soldiers of many colours.

And all this passes, in one form or another, across those few miles of sunshine and fields, to the dry-looking brown trenches, the trampled roads and tattered-looking trees and stacks, and at last to the terrible remnants of the short human tragedy, that lie for a while among the furrows and then for ever beneath them.

In a few months these battlefields which I traversed to-day may be part, if a small part, of history. The muskets we helped to carry back, packed among a few refugee peasants, may be in museums of honour.

To most of the men who died there, and made the names of these fields famous, their names were unknown. But for those who see them still only as ruined, littered fields, it is the dead, whose

names will be forgotten, who alone are present
in thought.

Meanwhile the troops are progressing up the
Marne. Our soldiers are in fine fettle. For the
moment at least there is respite from tension. As
I came back, away from the faint sound of guns,
through the heart of a thunderstorm, the clouds
broke in glorious wet mists of golden sunshine
over Paris.

Lagny, Friday.

Official reports to-day say that the Germans
have fallen back nearly forty miles from their
furthest point of advance at Coulommiers.
Also, that the British force has crossed the
Marne between La Ferté and Chateau Thierry,
and that the Prussian Guard has been rolled
back upon the marshes of Gond.

In so far as it goes this is correct, but the
news is at least two, probably three, days old.
The German right is retiring north and east,
upon Rheims, Oulchy-le-Chateau and Compiègne.
The British forces, upon whom has fallen the
brunt of the fighting at this vital angle, one
formed by the French line south-east from

THE BATTLES ON THE MARNE

Senlis and Nanteuil-le-Haudouin, and continued by the British north-east to Chateau Thierry, have succeeded in straightening the line, and thus eliminating the angle that gave us anxiety at the beginning of the battle.

It was the beginnings of the German retirement that I identified, when I approached from the north of Nanteuil three days ago. Its serious character is confirmed by what I have seen these last days from the south.

Starting from the north of Meaux to-day I recrossed the great bend of the Marne, by the help of a cattle barge that just held out for the crossing. It was doubtful what army we might find beyond.

It soon became evident that our official news was well behind the actual advance. Cannon were audible from the east-north-east. Near Torcy the battle was evidently going on.

Here and there, especially along the line of the Ourcq, were the signs of the progress of the week's battle of nations. The double lines of opposing trenches, hasty and scamped on the north (the German's). Torn-down stacks and stooks. Boughs and trees hacked down, across paths, or on the open roads. Branches lying in open mid-field, evidently carried forward as cover, and dropped for the final rush. Trees and stacks still smoking and black with fire.

A few peasants, with their carts standing by, were at the grim labour of interring the dead; charring the horses with fire before dragging them into the holes. Broken harness and accoutrements lay in little heaps, for removal. The old peasant women, with their brown, immobile faces tied round with coloured handkerchiefs, sat in the carts or helped. It is a grim task for many reasons; but the kindly rain has come to help. Bad for the men ahead of us, this rain, it will be worse for the Germans, in a hostile country, with more limited means of protection or remedy to be obtained from their base. And fever is beginning.

The peasants could naturally give little information as to the regiments or happenings. Only the broad facts could be followed. Near Ocquere, the ruts of advance and retirement of the German batteries, a shattered gun marking the firing position. East of Cocherel a mitrailleuse car, overturned, too broken up to be worth capture. But a couple of cheerful R.A. mechanics were at work on it, hopefully.

Round a much-perforated cottage, just to the north of St. Aulde, a fierce fight must have taken place. The furniture had been dragged out as cover, and on the summit of a trench, a hollow scraped in the hard soil, stood a large china crock, evidently set there by some cheerful trooper in derision of the German rifle-fire.

The sound of firing grew heavier towards Torcy, to our north-east, during the afternoon. Clearly a great battle was in progress. Impossible to approach nearer. We were already between our line in action and the French reserves who were holding the country behind, and forwarding up lines of munition wagons and supplies.

There were wounded in the cottages, the jetsam of the battle in front. But the line of the British communications was to our east, towards the Marne at Charly. We could get no news of the happenings in front. We were constantly challenged, constantly headed to the rear in some new direction. The men who passed us had the "battle look," the look on the face of Michael Angelo's "Dawn." I had enough to do to look after the personal factor in such an atmosphere.

And now we know what was going on there, across those little tributaries of the Clignon, at Torcy, a few blocked miles ahead. A thousand prisoners! Fifteen guns or more! The Germans fairly matched and beaten!

This has been no mere "blind," this rolling up of the German right, which we have watched with such anxiety. If their right was weakened, as I assume, to reinforce the armies in Prussia, they have paid for it. For they have lost, and lost heavily and badly; and at the corner, and against the little army which it was their desperate concern to break and overwhelm.

All I could conclude, as we forced our way back, was that the day was not against us. The movement of men was forward. The strange telepathic current that runs through villages long before reports reach them, was all of relief.

THE BATTLES ON THE MARNE

It was cheerful soldiers in blue who shoved my car on to the water-logged barge on the Marne; and, after a drift downward during which we scarcely breathed, it was laughing peasants who pulled us up on the far bank.

It is something to have been at least across the Marne and near on such a day, to have had the sound of those guns in one's ears, to have watched for the first time in five weeks' campaigning the forward movement of our armies.

The next morning, as soon as the barriers would let me pass, I was out again in pursuit of the receding armies. Day by day these flights became longer, and as the first glow of victory after the Marne battles passed into the deadly quietude of the long death grapple on the Aisne, day by day the difficulties of approaching the front increased. The easy smiling soldiers became again suspicious, and the constant challenges and " arrests " more numerous.

Saturday, with the pursuit.
North through Neufchelles again, and all but on to the banks of the Aisne. I had to leave the

car, because of vanished bridges, and get forward north and west on foot. I was blocked at last in the heart of an advancing column, resting in a half burned village.

The shells were bursting on the far side of the slopes. The French forces were coming up, and were dispersing as they arrived over the fields, distributing to the scattered positions. Far from our right and ahead there came the fainter sound of the guns of the British contingents, continuing the forward movement. They have advanced far since I approached behind their successful battle at Torcy. (This Torcy, on the Clignon, should not be confused with Torcy near Lagny, south of the Marne.) Occasionally, from the remote north-west, I thought I heard the echo of the same sound coming down the wind. If this were so, could it be that much desired enveloping movement from the west?

A few prisoners passed in carts. All with the herded, hunted, pallid look of frightened and exhausted men. Think of their start for this great march a few weeks back, amid the shouting and flags, and to the sound of the

perpetual vaunting, foolish processional —
" Deutschland, Deutschland über alles ! " And
now, lucky to escape the squalid wayside grave,
the little raw brown mounds all over the fields.
One or two, in the grey tunic, with the colourless
face and the bare head of the prisoner, were
hanging on to French officers' motors, acting as
grooms or mechanics.

Some men of the —— Regiment, carried
in the car, told me they had not slept for two
nights and days, though they joked heartily
enough ! It was not therefore a surprise to
see a number more dead asleep under a shanty.
I walked past two, who lay a little apart. One
stirred in his sleep on the stones. The other
was dead. But death is now too common a
shadow in this deadly mist of war, that drives
and condenses in trench and grave-mound over
the sunlit fields, to call for notice.

A little group of English artillery formed
another break in the monotony of fighting. They
were preparing for the reception of fifteen
hundred German horses just captured. Concerned
only with the care and cure of their sick charges,

they had no thought for the noise, turmoil, **and** incident of war about them. Give the **trained** man his own job, and he will see the world fall about him with only an absent glance!

Further to the east I was shown the site **of a** curious incident. Some deep German trenches ran down a slope from the road to a wooded hollow. Here some thirty rear-guard Germans had been captured. " We should have had 'em all, all the eighty, but the colonel was **too** kindhearted! He got one of our guns round and up there through that wood, just to sweep them trenches. And then he rode forward alone to ask 'em to surrender, some of them still firing at him! And most of them crept out there by the cross trench into the road again, and got away behind the rear-guard lot. You see how ? And one of the beggars we got had a gold watch ; and the colonel wouldn't have us take it **away** from him ! "

The conviction grew stronger and stronger, as I followed the lines of gradually accelerating retreat and obviously slackening defence, that cavalry, cavalry, is what we want to give the tired enemy no rest, and prevent them re-forming upon the supports that are being hurried from Berlin again on to this wing. Our own cavalry has done magnificently this campaign, and saved the critical days of retreat from Mons. If only they have been sufficiently rested and reinforced !

The French cavalry does not seem to have been always fortunate. It has too often timed its brilliant charges too late, and only swept over a crest when the German guns had got the range and could mow them down. Hence their support has not always been available at the right moment. But their courage and dash have been characteristic. Under a rocky knoll in a sloping cornfield which I passed on my return the line of one of these costly charges was only too clearly marked.

South, towards Lizy, a few peasants in carts were already dribbling back to their looted villages. The Prussians were here for a week or so and fought in the streets, using the furniture as obstacles. The destruction is pitiable. The châteaux were in many cases pillaged. Their gardens are strewn with bottles. The lawns are heaped with bolsters and palliasses. In one château, near Lizy, the orchard wall and trees were pierced and wrecked with shells in some prolonged assault, while over the opposite wall, commanding the deep little green lane alongside, a splendid mass of scarlet and orange lilies still glows triumphantly from the deserted garden.

In one such devastated village, between Meaux and May, a strange incident checked us. A dignified old peasant, wandering in the wreckage, was pouring out to me a passionate recital of wrongs. A son shot, a farm wasted, ruin before him. There passed a uniformed Government employee, with a dangerous, nervous face, who called out: "Be silent! The French have done us more harm than the Germans!" At such a time, in such a place, it was an insane outcry. Never have I heard such a torrent of execration as when the old peasant turned and sprang at him. Nothing but the vicious look and gestures of the younger man kept murder from being done. The incident was illustrative of the unbalanced mental condition to which war reduces the non-combatant. The younger man was himself ruined, and like a desperate, snarling fox he turned to hurt the nearest sentient thing, his more injured neighbour.

In torrents of evening rain I left the battle still continuing beyond the hill, and the two German armies being edged north-west through the forests of Villers and Compiègne, already in part behind the line of Soissons. So, back through the country north of the Canal of Ourcq. A few days ago it was in German occupation; now comfortably patrolled by Cuirassiers, in their rain cloaks; with watch-dog camps of infantrymen, cooking under straw shelters, cheerful and singing for all the torrents of rain and chilly wind. I am writing on an earth mound, on the wrong side of the Ourcq Canal. Some fifty sappers are hurriedly trying to repair the temporary bridge which we crossed this morning. It was frail then. Since then a huge lorry has gone through it. Eighty more of the great Paris omnibuses, now loaded with provisions, are waiting on the far side. It will never carry their weight, and we must get over first. We have done our share of work on the bridge, to earn an early passage. In the next field some soldiers are digging out the airman from under a fallen biplane.

The country has turned from a sunlight green to a dull grey with the passing of the summer; and there is an autumn mist of twilight heavy over the forests where the Great Machine is threatening to dissolve into its human elements, and confess its human limitations.

The feet in the proud Prussian parade to Paris are slipping, slipping, on the road.

Sunday.

Von Kluck's and Von Buelow's armies are still in full retreat; separated from the army of the Prince of Wurtemberg, with which they made a fragile connection by means of the Guard. The Guard themselves are perilously thrown back into the marshes of St. Gond.

This is the real thing. The men are fighting more feebly; the machine has become human; the cavalry horses—no longer the fine spirited Irish stock I had myself to dodge in Belgium a few weeks back—are worn out. It is pitiable to see the tired beasts loose and useless in the fields, or dead skeletons by the roads.

But the retreat has been fiercely contested. I followed to day the line of the battles north from Meaux, passing by those of which I have previously written; guided by the forward movement of troops and the traces of the retreating armies.

The retreat here roughly follows the line of the Ourcq. The battle has been fought with the French in desperate rearguard actions, at Vareddes, May, Beauval, Neufchelles. But nowhere can it be said an engagement began or ended. All along the road and through the adjoining fields it is the same terrible story— the trees scarred with shell, and the road littered with broken boughs: the fields scraped with hurried trenches: the stacks torn down for cover and holes scooped in their backs: the stark dead horses of artillery and cavalry lie in scores over the field and by the roads; and here and there still figures, or a cluster of figures in the German grey, still reproach the desolating injustice of war. The cyclists took a leading part in the pursuit, and scores of broken, charred frames marked where the German artillery found the range and caught their advance.

At every rise in the road, especially beyond May, more serious defences had been prepared. Fortifications of earth and squared stones between trees and bank; and here and there a deep burrow into the bank, bespeaking the human weakness that sought extra cover. And behind these earthworks, in the holes they left, lie the still figures. Fresh, shallow mounds, where the peasants have buried the fallen where they fell, run along the rim of the hard road itself.

The retreat, as it moved north, became almost a flight. Munition carts lie overturned, a machine-gun or two wrecked. Beside where the batteries swept the road, great piles of undischarged shells are still heaped, abandoned in the rush.

More tragic evidences were the scattered heaps of sleeping blankets, flung aside as the men were wakened by the rapid surprise pursuit. Broadcast, bottles and barrels; the Prussians, for want of food, seem to have looted the villages for drink. It was the same in Belgium. A pitiable piano, with the works shot away, stood in a field, with a dead man and dog beside it. The instantaneous stillness of a past battlefield is its deepest impression. Every grim vestige is suggestive of violent movement and sound, but it is all snatched into silence.

As I advanced, the long lines of wagons were still pouring up with troops and munition; happier now, and confident. The cannon sounded ahead from just over the fields, where the Germans have been forced back on the Aisne. I discharged a load of troopers and guns, and waited, listening to the thunder across the hill. It is more restful work. We have them! A few prisoners drove past us, blanched with nervousness and hunger. The wounded were being carted past to the Red Cross cottages. And still the flood of French supports is coming up.

From Crecy to Villers, from Villers almost to the Aisne, I have followed them now some thirty miles and more of savage fighting, of hurried retreat.

Monday.

Northward, northward! and now to the

east ; escaping one fatal trap by a most skilful
movement of tired men, but beginning in humbler
fashion to retread the wasted fields of the proud
parade from the frontier. So swift, it is difficult
to keep in touch with their retreat. Oho ! this
is a different business to fleeing before their
lightning march across Belgium.

And they are different men to meet, the stragglers and prisoners of the harried army, to the
perfect equipage of war I watched coming over
the hills, triumphant, into helpless Brussels.
Weary, anxious men, scarcely human, with mask-
like faces.

But you would steel your heart if you could
follow the tracks of their arrogant progress and
vengeful retreat. If you saw the deserted,
ravaged villages, heaped with the remnants of
the poor man's bare necessities. If you passed
through the tainted atmosphere of the countless
battlefields, that makes a sick offence of a country
of prosperous peace.

I came from the west into Senlis to-day, a
day after its evacuation by the Germans. A
detour took me through the Forest of Ermenon-

ville; the beautiful pine and heather glades and wide lakes haunted by memories of the humanist philosopher, Rousseau. It is haunted now by other ghosts. Impossible to suggest the eerie sensation of passing in utter silence through the village and forest spaces. Not a soul to be seen. Not a sound. But jettisoned along the road the dissolute debris of a vanished army. The woods cut for hurried defences. The houses wantonly broken and looted; and myriads of bottles, from the pillaged wine that served for food.

The desolation and silence prepared me for a shock. And it came. Senlis, Senlis of history, with its exquisite tower of open stonework and frame of romantic beauty, is a wasted ruin.

As I moved up the deserted streets, for a moment I was deceived. But every house, as I looked into it, was a shell; burnt out, skeleton-like, staring at the sky. Fire, and pillage, and ruin. And why?

The French soldiers held the last houses with effective fire. Then, for ten days the Germans held the town; and destroyed it, for amusement!

FROM THE TRENCHES

The Mayor and other elderly burgesses were set in front of the hotel, in single file, and shot with a single discharge, for practice. They were not allowed to speak to their wives and children, who stood by.

Proud of the fact, the General and his aide-de-camp have signed their names large in the hotel book—may they be kept, for execration!

The hostess of the hotel was forced to open every room, with a pistol held at her throat. The two old maid-servants who had stayed to look after the " great house "—now a smoking shell—were abused and injured. One wanders half an idiot in the village, still weeping.

Eighteen hundred bottles of champagne—they would have no other wine—were looted from the cellars. Double them, and you will not be able to account for the ankle-deep litter of glass in the streets. Hardly a house of importance is left with roof or floor. And how do you think it was done? Straw was piled. The tapers were stolen from the shrines and cathedral, and the soldiers amused themselves by throwing the lighted candles in at the windows of the houses. No wonder the small, crêpe-covered population is all in the streets. Here and there I saw a woman scraping in the burnt ashes, to clear a kitchen hearth, or look for some remnants. The station is a bleak ruin. Only the Cathedral tower, exquisite and light, protests against the sunlit sky.

But they were finely caught. The Zouaves, Chasseurs d'Afrique, who are pouring up through this country, arrived in trains of taxi-cabs between four and five a.m. The officer—no matter how he was occupied—fled out in his shirt; could not find his regiment; and was shot. The rest decamped—those who escaped. The prisoners I saw being sent back.

Not a crust is left in the neighbouring villages. At Mont l'Evigne the few surviving men snarled at the mention of bread.

You will hear with the less revolt of the horror I passed earlier in the day—some two hundred and forty Prussians, dead in one farm together, black and unburied, for want of peasants to bury them. They were killed by shell-fumes possibly, but had been bayoneted for double security.

FROM THE TRENCHES

It would be easy to amplify the details—the utter destruction of the houses, the stories of the insolence of the invading horde. The inhabitants, poor folk! are taking it with the quiet, deep indignation of a civilised people. Wagons of the wounded, of the American ambulance, passed in long train through the town, back from the front.

It was a relief to escape again into the broad green drives of the forest of Compiègne; to see only the abandoned German lorries, the scattered brown graves in the fields, where the horde were hunted back. In the forest we passed through miles of fierce brown Turcos, marching and resting. Their gorgeous colours and turbans, and fierce faces, a strange contrast to the deep shadowy avenues of the green forest. It was a greater satisfaction to follow the pursuit; to be the first from the outside world to greet the oppressed villagers and townsfolk; to hear in Compiègne the welcome " des Anglais !"; to listen to the women disputing whether " the Crown Prince " had really been there, and if it was he who escaped in half a uniform, and shot the

French Dragoon officer (who is lying in the hospital), when his pursuing cavalry arrived almost in time to save the bridge.

We followed them back, by the Oise, to the Aisne. The ambulances of our wounded kept on passing us. The fresh troops poured up in pursuit. But " one can breathe again now " was the word of the day, in village and town. We were barely an hour or two behind that hurried retreat. And there was no fighting. They had not stopped, or combined, to fight again—yet.

Paris, Tuesday.

As an instance of the working of the Machine the retreat of the German western army, with tired troops, has been almost as remarkable a feat as the great advance.

The hammer-blow at Paris was attempted, and checked as it fell. The second concentration of strength was launched on the west centre of the Allies' line. It only just failed, after a five days' struggle of almost superhuman magnitude. And now with lightning-like celerity the failure has been recognised, the strings of the armies

221

drawn tight, and the retreat accomplished with remarkable precision and pace.

At first the pursuit had to be conducted with forces almost as exhausted—men who had carried through the tremendous task of fighting a retreating battle for ten days, of converting it into victory and advance, and of then flinging themselves into the very different attitude of mind, and of manœuvre, demanded by rapid pursuit of a still unrouted enemy.

I have been out again to-day in the attempt to catch up with the march of return. The broken bridges, the abandoned wagons and munition, the stragglers, all speak of the precipitance of the northern-eastern wheel. The captured guns and mitrailleuses were being run back into Paris. The peasants and spectators' carts were loaded up with German trophies—undischarged shells, in their wicker cases. The ambulance wagons still passed, fetching in the wounded of both sides from the cottages, and even a few of to-day's fighting. But the provision for ambulance has proved altogether insufficient for the casualties.

THE BATTLES ON THE MARNE

The Germans have retreated upon a line of concentration where the armies of Von Kluck, Von Buelow and Wurtemberg can unite and present a new front, formidable enough to secure them the necessary rest for re-formation.

They never contemplated a halt south of the Aisne. It is beyond the river, on the Soisson-Rheims and Soissons-Compiègne curves, that their precautionary trenches were prepared.

Nothing gives a more definite idea of their own recognition of temporary defeat than the sight of their nearer trenches—abandoned without ever being used. The small wrinkle of earth and sods, with the spoon-shaped scoop for a single man behind, that they have taken to making for the retreat. Not so often as before the more elaborate continuous trench for a mass of men. They have learned a little of " open " fighting.

But they have hastened past them unused.

The Turcos and Zouaves are pouring up this line in great heart and hope. But the march is fatiguing, the roads heavier after rain.

In the villages and towns, Haramont, Coeuvres,

and others, the folk cluster round, stoic as ever, but easily smiling, hardly yet realising their release after the fortnight or more of terrifying oppression. In many cases they have been well used. The requisitions and regulations have been only those inevitable, from an invading army in hostile territory.

One curious but unimportant little coincidence in a day in which there is no great action to report : A week ago, I mentioned a curious scene in Beauvais, when through the silent, desolate town suddenly echoed the continuous blare of a horn, and a motor with two Prussian officers flashed through. Ten minutes later another car passed us on the outskirts of the town. This contained two other Germans, but this time prisoners under guard being carried back to Rouen. The cars did not meet ! The first car had an odd coloured wheel. Near Longport to-day I saw it again, wrecked by the roadside, the odd wheel high in the air.

As I looked out from the trees on the edge of the high plateau, the flat green valley of the Aisne looked untenanted, peaceful. For the present our cavalry have been naturally not in much better condition than the Germans. We have been unable to surround or outmarch to an extent that could convert repulse into serious defeat. They are far enough away, at any rate, to re-assure Paris. " Plus à Paris—plus à Paris ! " It is almost a tragic picture now—that of William II. watching on the hill by Nancy, in his white cloak and silver helmet ; the man who has been swayed by every psychic wave, romantic, religious, military, until he has brought an Empire totter-ing to the brink of ruin. Lohengrin above Babylon : the self-chosen emissary of an imagined providence looking out on the mirage of his promised land.

CHAPTER XI

On the Oise and the Somme

The armies were now fast locked along the Aisne. The varying fortunes of the first week made them impossible of approach. It was of interest to discover what was taking place on the German right and rear, where the position was still obscure, and the line of battle still indefinite and, therefore, easier of access.

Amiens, Thursday.

They are in touch again, and the German right is being enveloped.

It called for a long stroke from Paris to pass the wheeling left wing, for it was needful to avoid disturbing the intervening armies.

The journey through the Paris defences, those heedfully guarded lines that few civilians have hitherto penetrated on the north, was full of interest. By Neuilly and Pontoise we passed the careful fortifications, *chevaux de frise* of old railway lines crossed and pointed, sandbag forts, and the rest, all innocently couched under hedges of trees.

Every quarter-mile a challenge by different varieties of uniform. The peasants busy working at the trenches. For though Paris is regaining its own appearance, and the Parisian is even daring to begin to poke fun at his absent Government, there is no relaxation of watchfulness. "Until France is clear, and beyond, Paris is on guard!" Gallieni guarantees it.

I am getting accustomed to meeting odd company on the road. Three days ago it was General Gallieni and his staff, escorting two civilian Ministers round the battlefield, re-acquainting themselves with the new developments. Two days ago it was the Bishop of Meaux, in his lawn sleeves and violet biretta and robes, in a motor-car. To-day it came as an assortment of ——— officers, and a captured German pontoon train in wagons. At a railway crossing I was held up by a train full of German prisoners.

I turned east, skirting Creil and Pont, visiting the green glade and small brown graves that were said to mark the heroic charge of the Lancers, that first check to the oncoming tide upon Paris. Then back west to Meru, and north to Beauvais. Now and again the scarred walls of the end-houses of villages told where the Allies had fought on the great retreat.

At La Deluge—suitable name—an outlying farm was half burnt and in ruins. Here a small body of Germans had been wiped out by a French detachment in a six hours' siege. But an impassive farmer was leading his horses out of the ruins to resume work in the long-deserted fields.

Beauvais—and what a change! No longer the deserted city of a few widows running for shelter to the cathedral. Full of life, full of troops. We lunched cheerfully, at a freshly-opened hotel, on sheep's feet and pigs' trotters, with a jolly corps of French aviators.

The country is filled by our new army from the

west. Mitrailleuse cars met me every mile. Amiens is occupied by it. A few English and Scottish soldiers, punctilious to a point, delight the seminary students by saluting them as parsons in the streets.

The Germans left Amiens between Friday and Saturday, having requisitioned 100,000 cigars and drunk " only mineral waters," of which they have left their reckonings scrawled large on the tables.

It was one of the centres at which French reservists had to present themselves. Seeing the large number of men in the streets, the Germans issued an order that 1,500 men were to present themselves at six o'clock on the morning of evacuation, together with all the remaining motor-cars. In the dark morning they were marched off to dig entrenchments further east; and so far none has returned.

The Germans cleared the public hospitals, not the private ones, of all the German and French wounded. The French they treated well, but the " Turcos " they forced out of bed at the point of the sword.

FROM THE TRENCHES

Amiens has suffered little, except in pocket.

A yellow-haired hostess had us arrested here, as "Germans." One chuckled to see her returning to make vapid conversation after the betrayal— the Delilah! And one returned to her afterwards for another glass of coffee; for a courteous arrest is the assurance that we are again in the heart of a competent army.

All along the road I was warned that odd bodies of Germans were still about in the woods. As I swung east, for Peronne, I had the proof. South-west of Bray a shot or two on a wooded hill made us stop. It was too far away to be intended for us. A band of peasants, with a few dragoons, were methodically beating a wood for some stray Germans, firing and shouting, like beaters, as they moved through.

Presently four German infantrymen emerged at our end, with their hands raised, without arms. Footsore, frightened. We were made use of to run them back to Doullens, where they were transferred to an armoured car. It was a depressing drive. The beaten man is an insult to humanity, of whatever race he may be.

ON THE OISE AND SOMME

Some distance from Peronne the sound of firing sounded closer. I left the moving base, and part ran, part walked, about five miles forward and south-eastward. At last coming over a field, I lighted upon a small moving column of Turcos.

The officer, a large brown-eyed southerner, saw me first. He had no one to detach to go back with me, and was not unfriendly. It is a toss up whether troops of this type will embrace or shoot. Perhaps as a warning against temerity I was hurried forward to what appeared to be an odd end of a firing line. From the direction of the sound of the guns it appeared to be well on the right of a German position. Our extended line seemed to be overlapping them on the north.

With a number of my guard I crawled up and into a scanty trench, occupied by a line of some thirty Turcos. The next men gave our reinforcement a glance, but no more. On the actual line they have more important things to think about. The continual zip of bullets sang overhead. There was the wicked "bubble" of a machine gun not far to the right. The man

231

beside me talked continuously to himself. Two of the men further south presently slid forward against the breast-work, and leaned there motionless. In response, I suppose, to an order, my neighbours, who had been firing rhythmically, disappeared over the bank of the slight trench forward. I waited where I was, fortunately unheeded as I sat under the bank. The firing receded. I saw the backs of my friends disappearing into a wood in front. After a while, the Red Cross stretchers came along and picked up the two men near.

It was already late in the day. They came up, some dozen stretcher-bearers, under the direction of a young French surgeon, who was serving as a trooper, in uniform. I was engaged at the moment in some amateur bandaging, with the aid of a pocket Alpine surgical-case that has seen service in the Swiss mountains and in Belgium. They accepted me as an extra helper with little difficulty. Detained still, but allowed to help. Men at the front are concerned only with realities and their immediate work. An extra hand is an extra hand.

ON THE OISE AND SOMME

Along our trenches in the field there was little to do. The dead were left for later burial by the peasants. The seriously wounded were carried back, about a third of a mile, to where two Red Cross motors waited on a cross road. Another contingent was working from some fields on our left. A full ambulance ran past us as we came out on one trip to the road. It was all done very quietly and efficiently. The only raised voices were those of two men with whom the fever of bad wounds was taking the form of the furious raving of anger.

In most cases the Turcos were stoical and silent. One or two of the more lightly wounded had only to be helped back, after the first aid had been given on the field. One of them, as he limped along with his arm round my shoulder, hissed a whispered account of the exact form of death he designed for the next German he fought. It was chiefly gesture; and the dark brown face, close to my own, with the startling white gleam of the eye, gave it an almost theatrical ferocity.

In the dark it was decided to make a further search. My car, which a soldier was dispatched

233

to recover, was accepted to help in the task. It was a dark night, rather cold, but clear and starry. It was cheering to recognise the great planet which in Belgium we used to call the "Brussels star," because night after night Brussels used to stand in the streets watching it, never failing to recognise it as an approaching "Zeppelin." If you watch a star or lamp at night for long, it always seems to be in motion, backwards or forwards, up or down.

We crossed to where the Germans had retreated. The men carried acetylene lamps; two had electric flash-lamps, and another carried one of my car lights. It was a strange search, stumbling along the little pits of moist, cold earth in the dark. The lamps were masked, and flashed only occasionally, and downwards; and all talk was under the breath. It was uncertain that the Germans might not be somewhere near.

We stumbled upon five or six bodies, but the enemy had clearly had time to remove their wounded with them. Two, however, left for dead, had been revived by the cold of the night, and were groaning. We found them by the sound. They were back some way from the trench, in the wet grass. One had been hit behind the shoulder, presumably while he was retreating.

The dark chill of the night, with the little quick flashes of searching lights, and the mutter of occasional orders in the silence, lent additional impressiveness to the steady, business-like courage of the ambulance men. It is a work that requires very practised nerves under modern fighting conditions. None of the excitement of fighting for them, or the stimulus of " hitting back"; yet they get hit themselves often enough. These long days of furious bombardment, raking long lines of hidden positions, trench and village, must inevitably, and without intention, find shells dropping upon man, house or wagon, whose Red Cross is unseen or indistinguishable.

The greater credit to the men whose dangerous work and even occasional death can earn them no glory of individual exploit. Like the fishermen mine-trawlers in the North Sea, they are the nameless heroes of humanity on the edges of the shadow of inhuman war.

The firing began again before dawn, far to the south. When I left them, to convey two of the wounded Germans and an ambulance assistant back to the village, the surgeon and his party were getting hurriedly into two of the wagons, to follow up again behind the fighting line.

Boulogne, Friday.

Last night I crossed to England, returning early to-day in one of the worst storms conceivable on a Channel crossing. Boulogne and the north are beginning to simmer with a new movement.

The southern position is still stationary. The forcing of the Germans out of their strong defensive trenches is a question of time and of endurance. The French and British have the advantage of superior facilities for moving men or getting up reinforcements by rail.

It is still difficult to say whether the German right, as it lies, is fighting a stubborn rearguard action on the retreat, or if it is intended to hold its present lines. If the latter, it is in danger from the Allies' overlapping left, and from their movement on the north-west.

Our own troops would seem to be carrying again the burden of some of the fiercest fighting, about Soissons.

The region north of the German lines, which I traversed to and fro to-day, is a region of vague skirmishing, somewhat similar to that existing in northern Flanders. The Germans and French are alternately occupying the towns and villages near the frontier with small patrols or armoured cars. The Germans, on the whole, are contracting their web.

Lille is free for the moment, and either army uses it. The Cambrai neighbourhood is of course still German, on the line of their communications. The French are spreading up to the border again, in a gentle wave. The country is absolutely peaceful. The people go about their work in the fields with little regard for the wandering parties of war that go past on the roads.

It is a different sight from the deserted fields,

the panic-stricken peasantry, the hurrying troops, that filled this border when I came up last. That was in the week of concentration, after mobilisation, when I reached Valenciennes from Paris with a party of Belgian officers. They went to Maubeuge, I back to Calais. There have been flooding armies back and through that opening into Belgium since that week.

A few British stragglers still come in. A party of seventy with two officers, all in uniform, got through two days ago. Another courageous contingent of artillery came through with horses and men in fine condition. But the majority have been dressed by the peasants in the oddest of peasant remnants. They look hearty and bronzed, and the better for the holiday in the fields. In many of the woods further south German stragglers now take their place. The relations between these small unarmed bodies when they meet, both in strange territory, neither sure which should take the other prisoner, are pregnant with curious situations. Three Irishmen, whom the peasants hailed me to bring down from a copse where they lay hid during the day, told a tremendous story of stalking a German officer and knocking him off his bicycle. With a nice appreciation of their common position as outlaws, they then let him go.

For the moment we can but wait the issue of the long struggle on the Aisne. Of the greatest value would be the success of the French in penetrating the line on the east, against the German centre or left.

Another success on our left, valuable as it would be, would only force back von Kluck and von Buelow, accelerating their retreat, upon a new position on the frontier, without necessarily seriously defeating the combined armies. A success on our right would imperil their whole line, and cut off their retreating right wing in the Argonne. Under modern conditions, however, it is almost impossible for strategy to achieve the surprises which produce big defeats. The most we can look for, to end these long triturating battles, is the possibility of using more easy communications so as to be able to outnumber the enemy somewhere on the line, and so force a retreat by sheer weight.

This evening I ran all down the coast almost to Dieppe, and made the interesting discovery that all the coast towns, which only a few days before had been declared " open," and ordered to surrender all arms to their civic authorities, are again in military occupation. To follow the new development, I made, in the late evening, for Amiens, in violent wind and cold rain.

Amiens, Saturday.

For the present the news remains the same, —the continuation of a battle for positions, savagely contested ; the Germans fighting for time, time for the full use of their reinforcements and for the escape of their left wing in the Argonne region. The Allies are fighting to break the line on the east and to hold it, or turn it, on the west. Time, too, with its possible happenings in this quarter, is also in their favour.

We only hear of what is happening along the south front of the German army. About its south-west aspect there is a great silence.

ON THE OISE AND SOMME

The Amiens and northern German troops have fallen back upon a strong series of positions, which make an acute angle with those of their south front along the Aisne. Following the line of the Oise north, from the junction with the Aisne, they hold the line of highlands on either bank north to Noyon, thence west of the river to St. Quentin ; they cover the railway lines by Chauny, La Fere, etc., with Laon, as centre. Thence north to Cambrai.

It will be seen that their communications are exposed to attack from the west. The distances are too great for continuous protection in force. I have been able to-day myself to reach the railway line in two places, between Bapaume and Peronne, without interruption.

The country is more or less covered by cavalry and motor detachments, whose action is necessarily local. These are in turn hunted, marked down, or reported by the French and English motor-cars fitted with machine-guns. The game is exciting, and is succeeding in its object of condensing the German dispersed bodies. But there are signs of a more serious pressure from

FROM THE TRENCHES

the Germans beginning, that may eventually remove the centre of interest from the battle going on farther south.

The long-continued battle on the Aisne is in the nature of artillery duels, fencing for positions, followed by infantry attacks and counter-attacks on either side. So far we have had the advantage on the west, but at great cost. The counter-attacks by the Germans on our troops in the course of the nights have been repulsed with loss.

In the long business of wearing down we have the advantage, both in convenience of supply-service and in freshness and number of troops. But for a decisive issue, in view of the strength of the German position, we may have to hope for the entry of some new factor upon the scene.

The strong winds have dried up the roads to a large extent, and the movement of men and guns is again becoming easier.

In the region in which I have been able to approach the fighting, our counter-moves were proceeding vigorously and with plenty of confidence.

ON THE OISE AND SOMME

Amiens is in the overstrung, spy-mania condition of a town but just free of a hostile army, and again occupied by a friendly but mysterious military. As I ran in to-night in the dark, narrowly escaping driving into the river at the shattered bridge of Picquigny, I met the atmosphere like a thick fog. Sentinel challenges at every corner, suspicious civilian crowds thronging round if ever we checked. Two correspondents have been arrested as spies, and cannot be traced. To get myself and the car out without detention, I start to-morrow at the first light.

Creil, Sunday.

This has been a day of rather exceptional interest and incident. A number of hours have been spent in following up a line, and a direction, of which it has now become indiscreet to write in detail, but of whose possible importance to the issue of the battle of the Aisne and Oise those who have followed my account will be already aware.

That Von Kluck, if it is still Von Kluck on the German right, is alive to its importance, there is evidence in the strong reinforcements constantly thrust out towards the line Paris-Amiens, to anticipate the French movements, and in the vigour of the offensive which is pushing out to the west of Noyon. The conflicts between the patrols and our flying mitrailleuse-cars have made a distraction in the north to the unvarying character of reports from the long and terrible ding-dong battle on the Aisne and Oise.

Even the French papers are saying it to-day. "Keep your eyes also on the west. Don't be discouraged by the absence of material progress in that long-drawn conflict between the entrenched armies!"

That is all one may say after a number of hours spent in tense progress in sight and hearing of friendly and hostile forces. (*Note.*—I was following the development of the French encircling movement, by Clermont and Lassigny, round the German right wing.)

You are tired probably of reading about races with Uhlans. But they retain their freshness of excitement for the participants. I must add yet one more, and that happened only this morning. We were passing from Moreuil to Montdidier. Outside Braches the wreck of a motor car, the two hind wheels smashed by some sort of projectile, led to questions. It had been destroyed, seemingly for practice shooting, by a body of Uhlans who crossed the line last night. The three occupants had fled to the village.

The patrol was said to have gone on westward. Uhlans are very local in this wide, rolling country. Fifteen hours had intervened. They might be miles away. We ran on, with only a wary eye for the edges of the woods. The road, swinging up and down over the rolling, wooded slopes, ran up and over a crest, contouring round a grassy down-summit on a terrace which faced towards the west. The railway line and river lay below to our right. A long, straight road, bordered by tufty-topped trees, ran up along a sky-line to join our terrace-road from the west.

We were swinging slightly down-hill to the road-junction about a quarter of a mile ahead, when, quite a third to half a mile down the cross-road on the right, horsemen became visible, appearing and disappearing between the trees.

245

FROM THE TRENCHES

They might be a friendly patrol; but we put on full speed. It was soon settled. Some half-dozen broke into a gallop, or rather a canter, up-hill to intercept us. We had the advantage of slope, pace and distance to the crossing. The tilt of the hill and the road-bank also shielded us. I was only concerned about the moment of crossing at the junction, where we should be straight in view.

Some of the Lancers, some twenty in all, had halted and seemed preparing to fire. Luck favoured us. The half-dozen scattered men galloping up the road got in the way of the rest, and covered our crossing. We raced past, a good three or four hundred yards ahead at the junction. The road-bank and clumps of bushes again sheltered us, and a distant shot or two came nowhere near. It was rather joyous to turn and watch in glimpses over the bank the clearly irritated grey troopers pulling up their puffed horses.

We were still at full speed, in a sort of aftermath of excitement, some three or four kilometres further on and across the next rise, when

246

a placid green copse beside the road ahead suddenly grew alive, and a little swarm of men with bayonets moved quietly out to block the road. But the red and blue of the French army is visible afar. They greeted us from fifty yards off. "What have you seen?" We gave them the news. It appeared they were out on the trail of just twenty-five such marauders. Two came on with us to Montdidier to report. The rest marched off on a line that might cut ahead of our band. This is the railway line to the north, and for the last few days it has constantly been the scene of such little conflicts, on the one part the attempt to occupy the line, on the other to protect it.

In return for the news I was allowed to move up, under escort, and partly "requisitioned" for troops, nearer to the great battle than I hoped. First to Clermont, then by cross roads to Estrées; thence to near Giraumont, south-west of Ribecourt, which lies at an angle of the Oise northwest of the Forest of Laigue. From here, following a small cyclist contingent pushing their cycles, I got on foot through the woods on a track, until I could look down on the Oise. I did not see a battle. But, since it has been generally assumed that the Germans are east of the Oise, at least to as far north as Noyon, it was surprising to hear a very heavy cannonade proceeding from due north, showing clearly that the Germans were engaged well west of Noyon, towards Lassigny.

Where I was, however, the sight was all the more picturesque for the absence of the suggestion of destruction. The day had been squally, alternating silver streaks of sunlight and violent, windy rain. A silver shield of sunlight lay along the Oise to the north. The French were pushing up the western slopes of the river. At two points the troops, bright chequers of colour, were crossing on pontoon bridges. On the far bank they were trickling up in narrow streaks of colour again, into the green forest that swayed black with the wind. They were extending and supporting the French advance on this wing, which is pushing very gradually north, from as far west as Clermont, through the forest and fields towards the Noyon line.

ON THE OISE AND SOMME

The only signal of a battle progressing was the constant reverberation of guns that seemed to come alike from all quarters of the sky. I could identify only the peculiar uniform of the Senegalese and the light blue of the cavalry, as they moved past through breaks in the trees. Then the rain came down again, fiercely, and the scene lost colour in a grey drift of cloud and wind. Once so far up, and clear of the obstruction of bases, it was well to see all one could. Returning down the line of the Oise, and keeping in the woods, I got to the extreme west corner of the Forest of Laigue, where the Aisne joins the Oise. Most of the bridges have been blown up, and it is well not to approach those that exist, as things are.

Choosing a sharp corner, and retaining only what was essential for warmth, part wading, part swimming, I got across the Oise—it was decidedly cold—and followed at first the north bank of the Aisne.

The trees gave necessary shelter. It was a long and exciting walk, or rather stalk, east and then north through the forest, behind the French lines. All the traversable ways had to be avoided. The word " forest " gives a false idea of the open glades and blank stretches of country that give little cover. The firing seemed very near in front ; but it also seemed to be on either hand, confusingly.

A final long and enforced wait at last made it apparent that the sound was, if anything, coming nearer in this quarter. The Germans might be pushing a counter-attack southward, In any case, further progress would have been hazardous.

The retreat was like the advance. Glimpses of moving men through the trees ; long waits ; distant knots of ambulance men waiting, or moving southward. Always the confusing echo of firing, sometimes silent for intervals, sometimes clear and close as the south-west wind lulled. So back and over the Oise, with a big leafy branch to cover my drift across the river.

It was, frankly, a relief to rejoin my moving base, doing ambulance duty at Estrées, and to be on the clear road again. As I left the river, several barges of wounded were moving slowly southward. The little columns of Red Cross motors held the roads. This has been a terribly costly battle. We have held our own magnificently, but it has been against superior numbers, backed by accurate shell-fire from strongly-entrenched positions.

Unless the line can be pierced on the east, the great hope, thus limiting the Germans to the few lines of communications to the northern " troué," and unless their western lines can be seriously threatened from the north-west or in Belgium, we may look for a long, wearing winter campaign, a " stalemate" in the present positions. But a good deal has still to happen before we need make up our minds for that.

Creil, Monday.

I have been now once again making south, to resume contact with the battle along the Aisne. You have heard the account of the melancholy condition of the country north of and around Meaux, and of the ruins of Senlis.

Creil is in little better state. This was one point at which the tremendous German march upon Paris was first checked, to swing, with lost momentum, south and east, and then recoil.

The roads to the north and east bear the usual signs of past warfare. Wayside entrenchments, significantly enough often facing north-west, as if the Germans, when they checked, had half prepared to meet attack from that quarter. Hastily obliterated milestones and sign-posts. Villages with a house here and there destroyed. At Cauffry, for instance, the big Mairie is burnt out, nothing else touched.

Entering Creil from the north, at first only every house in four or five seems to have been injured. Further down towards the river, every second house; and then whole rows of empty shells, shattered by bombardment, burnt out with fire. Others still standing, with every window broken and the doors smashed in; pillaged and scooped out, as if by the enormous paw of some predatory beast. In the cold autumn wind and driving rain the inhabitants are sheltering in the empty frameworks, doorless, windowless, often roofless. The town is full of the usual tales of suffering. The boy scout, who piloted me, grew passionate over the long tale of a lady called *la belle Andaluse*. It embodied all the atrocities; with the single exception of the now dubitable anecdote of the "little boy who was shot because he pointed his toy gun at a soldier." For any one who has read the story of Napoleon's campaign in this district, in 1814, and of the Cossack atrocities perpetrated among these villagers, it has a grim meaning to hear, in 1914, their descendants in the same villages recounting, unknowingly, much the same catalogue of outrages. Civilisation will seem to bray at him, like a donkey running round in a well-wheel.

In the grey chilly evening the river dividing the town is a melancholy sight. The two twisted ends of the great girder bridge, blown up by the French on their retreat, droop into the broad river. Below this, still survives the remains of the German pontoon bridge, by which they crossed. A big ferry further down makes the only connection with the region northwest of the Oise for a number of miles.

None of the heroics of war in these depressing

after-views and moody, hopeless faces. A
column of French sailors swung through just
now; fine fellows, bronzed, and singing in time
to their springing step. It was more reckless,
more tuneful than the toneless, barbaric little
chant of the Cuirassiers as they rode past me
at Sombreffe in August. But that did not jar
with the sunlight and woods and the noise of
armies going into battle. Here the song seemed
garish and discordant, in the grey, miserable
awakening of a town to its own ruin.

And, if this of Creil, what shall we have left to
say of Rheims, or to think of its cathedral and
churches, reported to-night to have succumbed
at last to the week's bombardment? To German Culture—let Louvain be the memorial;
to the Imperial Piety—the ruins of Rheims.

CHAPTER XII

ON THE AISNE

PARIS was pleasantly tranquil. Folk were returning. The Boulevards had almost their traditional crowds. At the same time the long lock upon the Aisne, and the absence of news, had recalled something of the atmosphere of anxiety and doubt. Rumour was rife. In the usual attempt to check it, as well as to cover certain military moves, the circle of the defence was being drawn tighter. All permits were being cancelled. When I left Paris again, to try and regain the lines on the Aisne, it was with the knowledge that it would be necessary to take increased risks, with less chance of getting communicable news. If the position were to resolve itself, it would be on the north coast; as the result of a different development of the battle.

255

FROM THE TRENCHES

North of Paris, Monday night.

The army of the west that I have followed with personal interest through all its developments during the last weeks is now officially acknowledged as being in contact with the Germans.

Of the excitement of watching its growth and passage through the north of France, at Rouen, Beauvais, and Amiens, I shall be able to speak more fully when the official details as to its composition are allowed to be made public. "Keep your eye on the west" is all we have been able to say as reassurance during the two long anxious weeks of assault upon the profound German trenches on the Aisne.

And now, certainly not too soon, when the Germans have extended themselves once again in desperate efforts to break through on the south at Soissons and Rheims, comes the threatening pressure of the new army upon their lines of communication to the north. Have their reinforcements, brought from Belgium

256

and the Argonne, come up to check it in time ?

Nor is this all. We have all deduced from the German activity lately the movement westward and northward of the French troops on our left wing, up past Clermont and Lassigny. This has of itself been gradually overlapping the German right. Now it forms a single enveloping arc with the forces pressing in upon St. Quentin.

It was only when the magnificent fighting on the Aisne made it clearer day by day that the Germans were fairly held in the south that such a movement of troops became justifiable. We could reconstruct now where these troops were drawn from, and the moves of the splendid game that the Allies have played. But that must wait until the game is played out.

Meanwhile that fearful sacrifice of life upon the Aisne two weeks ago, fighting unparalleled in history for severity, has gained its object. Time has been won for the one move that serves to hook the Germans out of their immense entrenchments. We start the third week of the battle with easier breath.

There have been many rumours that the Germans were really further south on the line of the Aisne than public information acknowledged. There were sections of the line about which nothing was known, and not only that mysterious west.

It is possible we may hear later that there were anxious days last week, when Rheims was not the southern boundary of the Germans, nor yet Soissons; and that some of the ground now slowly won at great cost has but been regained.

It was to clear this up that I spent to-day travelling behind the whole line from Rheims to south of Compiegne; approaching it at the vital points, so as to define the German position. Although there had been German cars imperilling the road, it proved to be only some of their reckless skirmishers. We got through, without a rumour of them, to the heights south of Rheims.

ON THE AISNE

Passing thence east, it was not difficult to place, from sound and sight, that the Germans lay well east of the town; and that, with the duel taken to-day more easily on both sides, the French were assailing them upon the heights of Nogent l'Abbesse.

Their loss of the height of Brimont, on the east, prevents the French making use of the Canal of the Aisne and Marne, or the adjoining railway. At the same time, the French retention of the line of heights of Craonne on the west commands any advance of the Germans upon Rheims by this route.

Circling away from Rheims to the west, I came up south of the Aisne and the Craonne heights, by Poncherry and Montigny. Here I met a train of wounded and some stragglers in the village, who told me of the sustained assault that is being made upon the French positions; the Germans making charge after charge, even with the bayonet, but being repulsed with great loss.

It is obviously vital for the Germans, with

12

the growing pressure on their flank, to break through on the south, and, by threatening Paris and separating the armies, to force a withdrawal of troops from their communications.

I was near enough to the Aisne to be able to see the character of the country on the far side, which has cost both Britain and France so dear to assault. A gradual slope of about half a mile up from the river, steepening into scarps and wooded heights, and dotted with white quarries. These latter were held by the Germans deeply entrenched, and their guns commanded the passage of the river.

Driven at last over the edge of the hill, they returned again and again in massed charges, and were swept away by our men, more lightly entrenched, high up, just under the brow.

To the west of this, as far as Soissons, the two weeks fighting has mostly consisted of long-range artillery duels, across the river and, later, over the heights. The Germans, better

ON THE AISNE

hidden, and with longer range, shelled our slighter trenches with fearful accuracy.

About Soissons the British resisted successfully a concentrated assault of more than a week's duration, certainly not less in savage determination than that upon the French around Craonne. Our cavalry especially distinguished itself.

Several men wounded, or resting from the front, in these villages, told me the same story: " It began about six—heavy, accurate shell fire ; there was a lunch interval ; it stopped about dusk every day. Then in the night, often came the charges. One night I couldn't count them ! It was awful. Kill, kill, kill, and still they came on, shoving each other over on to us ! "

No man but had his story of comrades on either side shot or smashed day after day, of the shriek of shells, of the perpetual groaning of the wounded as they lay in the wet trenches. " Seven days and nights of it ! and some nights only an hour's sleep." And all the same

261

description—"It was just absolute hell." No one found another word to describe it.

And the sight of the men bore it out. Muddied to the eyes, soaked, often blood-caked. Many were suffering from the curious aphasia produced by the continuous concussion of shells bursting. Some were dazed and speechless, some deafened. And yet, splendid to relate, I saw on no Briton's face, wounded or resting, the fixed, inhuman stare of war. Even the wounded were in good spirits, unconquerable,— the sporting "looker-on" attitude of the British soldier.

I scrawled a line of letter for some of them; they all wanted it said that it had been "hell"; that they were glad to be out; but not sorry to have been in. Many wanted advice added to "brother Tom" or "cousin Dick" not to rush into it; but they knew themselves, as anyone who knows the breed would know, that it was just that scrap that would make Tom or Harry mad that he had not been in it too!

The French were more absorbed and aloof, less of "professional" fighters. They could not do without the personal touch. A little group of the Line sat before a burnt cottage sharpening and caressing their bayonets—"Rosalie" they call them, for love of their blood-stained edges.

Soissons has suffered little less than Rheims. Not from fire as yet, but six or more dark, jagged holes showed where the cathedral has been shelled. The town looks more than half in desolate ruins.

The fighting here has been indescribably fierce. At Bucy-le-Long, just to the north-east, the Germans dropped shells into a school converted into a Red Cross ambulance, killing many wounded. One of the wounded assistants described the scene. "They didn't intend it, probably; we had troops coming up just behind, and they're poor shots!"

Description of the sights and sounds of past battlefields are monotonously grim, and useless to repeat. But the villages and country in the track of this long battle, along the south of the Aisne, cannot be left unmentioned, if war is to be recognised as reality.

To move here is to move in a country of

FROM THE TRENCHES

abandoned trenches, half used as graves; to move through the tainted air of the unburied; to see the countless dead, broken life, broken humanity, burning, or being thrust, with the fortunate callousness of the peasant, into trench and pit; to meet at every turn some deadly reminder of mortality; to see every house and field flecked with some pitiable wreck or litter of battle. The details need not even be imagined.

But the wounded, as I saw them, returning in car and train, lying in temporary shelters or waiting their turn at wayside stations, are at once a more painful, more real reminder. British, and French, and African, side by side, patient, courageous, appreciative of the little help that can be given by the few hands. It is the one sight that can still move one—that look of youth and hope struck out of the face of the young soldier, the dulled expression, of just clinging on to consciousness of life, that alone survives.

At Villers Cotterets and Crepy I saw and talked with many of them; but not for news of their exploits. We shared a common weariness of war-talk—the details were too present; and most of them characteristically, when they had asked for news about " the victory," spoke most of the peasants, and the hardship and suffering they had seen in the villages; very little about themselves or the friends they had seen killed.

South of Rheims, Tuesday.

With even more difficulty to-day we made our way up again into the battle region. Rheims was the first object. I managed to get to a point where I could look down and out at the city from its southern heights. Picture it for yourself, the long, rolling, wooded circle of hills, the broad green plateau of trees and houses, dipping to the irregular town; and in the centre, an immense landmark, the high, grey cathedral, with its two crowned towers of elaborate stonework.

At the first view, in the grey daylight and the roar of the wind, nothing seemed unusual. The outlines of tower and town looked as before. Then I put up the field glasses, and in a second the sight fell to pieces, with the sudden incongruousness of the destruction of Pompeii or Jerusalem as we see it on the coloured moving pictures, when the walls fall flat under red artificial flames, and in a second the towns remain only geometric sections of black ruins.

The roofs were there, but shattered into dark caverns of bombardment. The gables stood, blank, and with windows transparent to the sky. The streets, scarred white or in dark hollows of crumbled brick. And the Cathedral? The walls were standing, the towers, and much of the roof, but blackened and defaced. The towers, blurred in detail and fractured. The windows, with tracery shattered, and blinking as it were painfully at the unusual daylight that streamed in upon the black ruin of the nave.

And over all the grey haze of conflagration, mixing in one dark overhanging curtain with the yellow pestilent fumes of past bombardment.

Beyond, on the further heights, the grey sky was seamed with the spurt and smoke of occasional bursting shells; and the ear, guided now by the eye, could distinguish from the rush of the wind the single explosions of the German shells and the nearer crash of the hidden French batteries, as they responded, firing across the hill at the unseen army.

I would not, even if it had been easy, have approached nearer. Details of destruction could add nothing to the realisation of these monstrous reactions of war. This was, to myself, the second conscious shock in all the two months of warfare—Louvain was the first. The sight of dead and shattered bodies soon passes unrealised. There is nothing of the man who lived, even if we have known him well, left in lifeless remnants. What he meant and what he produced are no longer there. But to see a dead or an injured child, a mutilated work of art or thought, is to see the murder of men's souls: the defacing of the ideal which men live and die to conceive, to embody, and to leave as their contribution to the eternal principles of beauty and continuance.

FROM THE TRENCHES

What has provoked this wanton, deliberate destruction ? The anger of disappointed, hungry, chilled men in their realisation of failure and fatigue ? The revenge for the death of some popular commander, some General von Revel, von Rapine, or von Ruin ? Who can say yet ? On the spot there seemed to be no " military " excuse, of tactics or precaution. It looked like the irresponsible outrage of a tipsy child with a heavy hammer. Whatever the conditions of ultimate peace, let us see to it that the hammer of ponderous armaments is forced from Germany's hands. The " philosophical Teuton brain " may then have time to clear itself of the fumes of a reeling militarism.

The tapestries have been buried. It is reported that the treasures of the Cathedral are safe. Why, O why, was no effort made to remove the priceless windows in time ? We did it in our Minsters as long ago as the seventeenth century, before the threat of bombardment ; and the confidence in German " culture " cannot have been so deep-rooted !

I was glad that I could not see the injury to the famous " rose " window in the west front, through which the sunset used to colour the pillars of the nave with a marvellous amber and gold light.

As I passed by the town I met the venerable Cardinal Archbishop, in his robes, a strange contrast to the knots of uniformed soldiers and the few darkly-dressed, depressed inhabitants. He reached Paris, from the Conclave, two days ago, and, impatient of the absence of news, has come out to see for himself what has befallen his cathedral ; and that in spite of the German raiding cars, that have fired on passengers on the roads from Paris yesterday and to-day, and of the proximity of the cannon. I took off my hat to a very gallant man.

But a week or so ago I stood up and cheered the grand old Bishop of Meaux, when, as one of the first civilians to get into Meaux after the

FROM THE TRENCHES

battle of the Marne, I found him, in violet robes, still going gently round, looking after his few surviving flock. He, almost alone, had refused to leave the town, and endured all the risks of the encircling battles and the indignities of the German occupation.

The Germans have made no exception of priests and professors in their "disciplinary executions," and now that they have started on the cathedrals—first Louvain, then Malines, then Rheims, and now Soissons—a bishop who stayed to face them showed a good man's courage.

Wednesday.

In a village south of Rheims this morning I was delayed for some time by the passing of a column of German captives, being brought down from Craonne by the French. There must have been more than a thousand in this single division. Some of them were big fine fellows; a number quite lads; all looked pallid and with the strained look of fatigue and hunger. A few were allowed to sit a while by the road, to rest sore feet.

Those to whom I spoke, allowing for the fact that they were frightened and probably anxious to propitiate, confirmed the impression that the Germans have lost very heavily and are in sore straits for food. They spoke of the practical destruction of whole regiments, more especially in the assaults round Soissons and Rheims. To the audacity and omnipresence of our airmen, and to the accuracy of our shell-fire on their trenches, their accounts bore constant witness.

One lad, a " Sextaner " in an Ober-Realschale, was allowed to rest for some time, and soon began to talk quite cheerfully. He showed me his pocket diary, a strange little document. It contained chiefly the notices of his messing together with six or more of his chums, and of the rare additions of food other than rations. On later pages came the little notes of someone missing in the evening. A few new names were added. These, too, disappeared. Finally, almost

271

the last entry, of four days ago, came the sentence, " Remains only Max and me." But Max was not with the prisoners.

At certain of the base villages as I followed the line south of the Aisne, I saw other prisoners, active and willing as ambulance orderlies. They were already moving about cheerfully—the French are most kindly captors—but none of them had lost the stamp of pallor imprinted by the exhaustion and strain of that prolonged fighting march. Not one but was tired of the " useless war." It is only the stay-at-homes who have not lived in a war atmosphere, for whom it retains its colour of heroics after a few weeks of its squalid realities.

I crossed the Vesle, on a pontoon bridge, and visited two of the seven bridges which the Germans destroyed as they retired before the British over the Aisne near Soissons. A south country Briton told me the story of that first crossing.

" We were the advance division. We got there at nightfall, a desperate long march. The

ON THE AISNE

Germans had dynamited seven out of the eight bridges, but one just stood. We were ordered to shuffle across it singly, at ten yards intervals. It began at midnight, in the dark, a queer, nervous job; and we weren't all over, quite, by five in the morning. Two of the chaps slipped in, astray in the dark, one just ahead of me. I thought it was the bridge going up—the sort of ' plump ' he went ! "

I have had that feeling several times these last weeks, the stealthy crawl across the bridge with dynamite already laid below it.

North of the forest of Villers, the region which is a grim cemetery of men and of the homes of men, full of the smoke and dust of ruined houses and of the smoke and dust of burning piles of what were men, many soldiers were still lying on straw under shelter from the rain, waiting their turn to be fetched down by the ambulances. There are scores still waiting.

For one I took down a letter. This is its substance : " Jack and me were in that show

FROM THE TRENCHES

at Shivers (Chivres-sur-Aisne ?) It was not man-fighting that week ; just banging with engines over our heads, and getting them too, often enough.   When it got dark, 'they' always rang off.   And we went out, not under orders, just for our turn ; about six of us. Jack got a sentry—here—and we got to the pit ; but they were on us before we could mess the gun ; and it was pretty fair hell in the dark ; just jabbing at anything you heard or touched.   Three of us got back ; and we left 'them' some burying to do on their own, too."

The valley of the Aisne has a deadly sameness. At Retheuil and Chelles, the silent apathetic peasants—all too few—were heaping remains of men and horses for burning, or dragging them into the long raw trenches that scar the fields with white issues of lime. Anything of value or metal is dragged off, the bodies thrust in, and, for all the pestilent air, the peasant stolidly munches at his bread between whiles.

It is astonishing how little it affects one after

a day or two. I don't believe the sight or sound of always present death, or even, for that matter, the more intolerable affliction of sleepless nights, wet trenches, cold winds, and continuous strain, has taken five minutes of his quaint optimism from the British soldier. And yet this war is being fought without the exciting accompaniment of bands or drums. There are no parade sights ; no colour.

It is almost impossible to get the names of their places of past adventure from the soldiers. The French names, if ever heard, are soon forgotten. It is exciting to them even to hear that they are near Paris. They date from " where So-and-so got hit," or " where we got those fags from a hofficer," or where " the women ran out to give us drinks as we rode by." Very often the name survives as a mysterious village called " Ralentir." (Visitors to France may remember that this is the big notice put up outside villages, the "Drive slowly" warning to motorists.)

It was curious to recall, as I looked north later

in the day towards Vic-sur-Aisne, that I got
almost as far as this a fortnight ago, after the
German retreat from Meaux, thinking I was
well behind our armies, and found and
smoked in, their line of abandoned trenches,
in the company of two incursious peasants. The
Germans were even then making their huge
entrenchments on the hills ahead, and it was to
cost a fortnight's fearful fighting before our
men made good their position on my seemingly
lonely slope of fields.

We were " requisitioned " again, to run to
Mont St. Marc. As I looked across at the
Forest of Laigue, I knew now that the check
that turned me back in those woods last week,
after swimming the Oise, was one of the violent
counter-attacks by the Germans; when they
ventured, as they rarely have done, to charge
with the bayonet.

On that same day, the bombardment which
I heard from the direction of Lassigny, proves
now to have been the beginning of the French

resistance to the German advance in that quarter against General Castelnau.

At Crepy, on the return, a Turco, whom I must have met at the fierce skirmish south-east of Peronne, recognised me as he lay, a strange figure white with loss of blood under his African tan, his turban and brilliant uniform blood-stained, waiting to be moved into an ambulance car.

" Ah, they got me for a time, not long "—it was odd French—" but I assisted two with that, first (the bayonet), and then there remained to me these " (a significant gesture of the hands).

A badly-wounded north countryman, who lay beside him, with a nurse temporarily bandaging his shoulder—another shrapnel wound; they are nearly all shrapnel wounds—evidently understand the gesture, if not the lingo. " Fine chaps at a scrap, the darkies. It's funny, though, I couldn't use hands like that; sort of claws fashion. Now I could go on with a fist— this way—all day; just smash them. Some difference in education, d'you think ? Or just natural ? "

The nurse stopped the speculative opening. But think of it ; in the surroundings ! Our undefeated British soldier, tolerant of the individual, critical of the " foreign ways," ready to argue an abstraction, to fight, to make or be turned into a joke, even while every breath was a painful effort.

Thursday.

There has been a lull in the fierceness of the struggle along the Aisne, which is developing into the Battle of the Rivers. (*Note :* I believe this to have been the first time this name was suggested.) The lull is doubless not unconnected with the great changes of front in progress. Some days ago I was involved in the movement of the French forces round the left wing by Clermont ; later, to-day I was to learn from an airman of the even greater rapidity with which the Germans have poured their reinforcements, and their army from the Vosges, on to the line of the Oise towards Peronne. (It was the mass of these troops, and the rapidity of their swing across on the inner lines, that enabled the Germans to anticipate the Allies' move and, for a time, even push them back at certain points, at Lassigny, Chaulnes, and Peronne, as we now learn from the official communications.)

To-day was my last visit to the lines on the Aisne, the last opportunity of seeing something of the actual fighting. We reached Fismes early in the day, and, as there were rumours in Paris that the Germans had penetrated south in this region, we were relieved to find an extremely peaceful landscape. Only the usual traces in the villages and on the fields of past fighting.

Here fortune favoured us. For several weeks we had been inquiring in vain on all our excursions for a certain French regiment of the line, which contained the much-loved brother of my friend and driver. At Fismes we came by chance upon a small section of his company, who were escorting some wounded. We fraternised at once; and

they told us where we should find him, engaged
in the trenches across the Aisne. Not only this,
but they gladly took advantage of the car to
run four of them back to their advance post, or
rather as far as was permitted us, under their
helpful escort.

On foot we traversed the last fields to the
bank of the river. The appearance of this grim
border region of past battle, the burnt cottages,
scarred fields, blackened trees, and the faintly-
marked trenches and pyres of the buried and
incinerated dead, has been already described.
There is a terrible monotony in such scenes.

The Aisne was crossed on a light pontoon,
for foot soldiers only. I will not specify the
point nearer than to say that we were behind
a notable junction of the allied armies. A low
spur, rather exceptionally tree-covered, came
down close to the bank on the far side. In a
temporary base-camp, of shelters and enlarged
trenches, under the spur, the much-sought
brother greeted us, and a very cordial welcome

was given us on his account. A lieutenant was in charge, who invited us to share the combined rations.   The staple was a loaf of bread, hollowed out and filled with some very highly scented sort of tripe ; apparently a popular and certainly a filling meal. Actually, too, hot coffee in pannikins.   We contributed the usual cigarettes and journals.

The lieutenant did not see his way to letting me go forward, although the German fire on our trenches ahead had ceased for some time, and the only sound of guns came from some distance away, in the direction of Craonne. The time passed, however, unnoticed, in the interest of watching the movements of sections passing and repassing the river, in relief or support. Twice a number of wounded were carried past and over the bridge. They were still being collected, or brought down, after the desperate German assaults by night and day that preceded the lull. Three small detachments stopped in passing, moving up to the front.

FROM THE TRENCHES

They were all sun-browned, rough-chinned men here. Some had been in the trenches for a week or more, and looked fine-drawn and battered. They were uninterested but confident. Not the sort of gallant gaiety and glitter we are accustomed to associate with the traditional French soldier. That, if it survived the parade times, has given place to a serious intentness upon the one idea, a kind of setting of the teeth to face the issue and force the victory. For the French soldier has more imagination than ours. He has to make up his mind not to picture to himself results and effects which our men simply disregard, as not part of their particular professional concern.

The stories they told had necessarily great resemblance. Of hours of crouching under well-directed shell-fire. Of men killed or decapitated beside them, of hairbreadth escapes from shrapnel, of confused night attacks, of the joy of using " Rosalie " upon the hated grey bodies, when at last they got the chance. And, above all, of the continuous, dreadful noise of the guns and of the shells passing. Several were partially deafened or stupefied by the concussion. A few told of comrades who, not from failure of nerve, but from the mere physical, shattering effect of the perpetual roar and scream upon more nervous systems, had had to be sent back for a time from the line. And "spy" stories, as numerous as ingenious.

After an hour or so the "brother" had to go up to take his turn in the trenches with others. Our officer had gone off in the interval at a summons; and the sergeant left in charge—we were now firm friends—agreed to let me go up a specified distance for a certain time with the section moving out.

We turned to the right round the end of the spur, about thirty of us, ascending diagonally up the side, with a parallel valley receding below us. I had been given directions as to how we were to take advantage of the natural cover, and in places where we should have been more

283

exposed to observation from heights or airmen this cover had been very ingeniously supplemented.

The firing from the greater plateau towards Craonne grew more distinct, but even so it seemed to be none too vigorously prosecuted. The cautious approach along the wet green slope towards a real, if distant, enemy, revived the feelings of keen excitement of our man-hunting game in the Lake Fells. But in the valley bottom, and occasionally on our slope, there were harsh reminders of reality in the pits of shells, broken trees, the litter in abandoned trenches, and here and there the unburied German dead. A number of peasants were engaged in removing these last traces, in the more sheltered depressions. But, as the corporal explained with a shrug, " What would you ? If they see where we are, they fire. We cannot risk the good living for *those* ! "

All too soon, as it seemed, we reached the advanced point where on an upward slope, the

work of pushing forward diagonal trenches was
going on.   On our left the hill hid the view;
but across the valley, on the right, the same
active, methodical work was just visible in the
slight stir and occasional glint of mattock or
red trouser.   With a gesture my attention was
drawn to a carefully concealed battery.   I
doubt if I should have seen it for myself.
" They haven't marked that down yet; that's
for a surprise when they begin again ! "

We crossed a system of narrow man-deep
galleries, well-covered, and which had evidently
been heavily shelled.   I was hurried forward
through this, now with even more caution.
" They've got the range of this; but we're out
there now ":—and the " brother " indicated a
point a third of a mile ahead, where, it seemed,
a sap was being carried forward, on a zigzag
towards the crest.   Just as we were advancing,
the unmistakable moan of an aeroplane sent us
to cover, under the old entrenchment.   I failed
to see it; but a sudden outburst of firing on our

left, that died away again, gave the line of its passage. "You may expect something here, after that—— has been over," was the remark, made to me, I think, with half malicious intention.

In a small pit or field-quarry on the slope, of innocent appearance, but in reality converted into a very adequate straw-lined shelter or base for the men engaged in digging beyond, I was left; while the section moved forward to take the places of others. These, when they came down, would see me back again. I saw the "brother" leave me with regret. My companions were four men and a corporal, rather glum and tired, but not unfriendly. Two had been slightly wounded, but had refused to go down.

We had barely got on to terms, with grateful cigarettes, when a single growl echoed across the slope in front; and the unmistakable crescendo whine of a shell passed high and to one side above us. It was followed by another, which

shrilled its menace more directly overhead;
and the flat, quaking explosion, hitting the ear
like a blow, could be heard further down
over the slope. The men paid scarcely any
attention. "It will not go on; we shall not
reply," said one. "Reassure yourself: it is at
our old trenches," added one of the wounded
men, with half a grin. The sensation of being
shelled over is denied to the civilian; and in
my own case the opportunity was probably
unique. I risked the reputation for unconcern
of the race, and crept out and up under the
higher lip of the depression; from here, well
sheltered, I could look backward and down the
slope.

Four more shells passed in quick succession.
The roar of the discharges rolled in a continuous
echo back and across the little valley; through
this the singing scream of the shells stabbed
venomously. One fell beyond the old trenches,
and exploded in the ground—I saw the huge
shattered cavity as I returned. Two burst

accurately, man high, over the earth-works, faced with sods, of the abandoned gallery; the sight and sound were indescribably shocking to the unaccustomed eye and ear. The last did not explode, but, from the spurt of earth, buried itself deeply twenty yards nearer me up the slope.

As I had been told, no reply was made in this quarter, and no more followed the six. A quarter of an hour later the returning section came back; and again, with an escort of twenty dumb, earth-stained, and hungry blue-coats, the cautious return was begun. As we got down the caution was dropped. " They don't want it to-day any more than we do "—and we clustered in a quick walk back to the base.

As an impression of the futility of warfare, the sight of this useful manhood, designed to dig a fruitful soil for profitable living, now burrowing for life in barren trenches, was sufficient. As an impression of its hideous trespass, the intrusion of those discordant shells, shrieking

over the sunlit hill with a sort of murderous
absurdity, splitting the still air into shreds of
hateful noise, and vanishing against the motionless trees in drifting clots of sickly green vapour,
was all complete. If further proof were needed,
it lay about me in the melancholy accidents of
destruction, scattered over the " no man's land "
that I recrossed on my return. The whole suggestion was of some recent, sordid violent orgy,
by a party of criminal tramps, in a peaceful
garden.

Many of the bridges were broken down, and,
after rejoining the car, we had to make a wide
sweep to the west. The roads were blocked by
the wagons and columns of the French westward
movement. I passed again through Crepy and
Senlis, and round west of Clermont, which was
obviously in the agitated condition peculiar to
a military occupation. The distinctness with
which the guns could be heard from the St. Just
road, suggested that the Germans had advanced
considerably to the west, since I had last heard

them from the south of Lassigny. From Montdidier we turned east, hoping to get to Roye;
but it was getting late and the road became
hopelessly congested. An aviator whose machine
had been injured and to whom I was able to
give a lift, told me that he had seen the German
reinforcements pouring up in very great numbers
behind the Oise; and it was clear that, for the
moment, their possession of the inner lines had
given them the advantage in forming on the new
front.

Through by-lanes west of Roye we made
towards Rosiéres in the dark, hoping to hit a
main road back towards Amiens. We were
stopped again by the sound of firing in front
and a little to the east. Before turning back
we determined, if possible, to discover its meaning. Leaving the car in a field, the driver and
I walked forward cautiously through the woods
in the direction of the sound. We were in one
of the big hangars of large forest trees that crown
the crests of the rolling uplands in this district.

ON THE AISNE

As we came out of the wood, and just across the crest, there came a sudden crackle of rifle firing from the trees on the opposite crest, about a mile and a half, so far as I could calculate in the dark, to the east. For the moment it was difficult to account for it; but the driver suddenly called my attention to some little sparks of flame in the dark sky. They seemed to be dropping on to the far wood. The reason at once suggested itself:—a daring German airman, making a night flight, had located a detachment of the French in the wood, probably by their camp fires, and was dropping little balls of flame to give the range to his associated battery. A few minutes later the dull boom of heavier guns, firing from a greater distance, which continued for some fifteen minutes, and then ceased, made our speculation a certainty. It was a curiously suggestive glimpse; the darkness lit and broken for a moment, declaring the presence of the unceasing, sleepless strife.

It was clearly not possible to force our way

further north ; and, as it was now too late to gain entry into any town of shelter, we spent a not uncomfortable night, sleeping in and beside the car. With the first light we turned west and south, and regained Paris almost as soon as the gates were opened.

CHAPTER XIII

The Shadow of the War

THERE could be no object in making further visits to the deadlock along the Aisne. The German advance, which I had followed across Belgium in the beginning of the war, and met again where it shattered upon the Allied position east of Paris, had failed. Their rapid consequent retreat on to the heights of the Aisne, and the reassembling of their armies, had been successfully accomplished. Both sides had been unable to convert the end of the first great move into decisive victory or defeat, and had dug themselves, after desperate initial efforts, into impregnable entrenched positions. The serpents of war were dragging their slow coils west and north, seeking more open ground for a fresh grapple.

FROM THE TRENCHES

The new development had to be looked for in the north. Time must elapse before it could take definite shape. The first phase of the war was ended.

In the interval, before the next began, like a foiled snake drawing in its head and thickening its coils, back in Belgium the huge length of the German army was beginning slowly to swell itself out, forcing the last of the unhappy population out of town and village, to the coast, and to the sea itself. For " military reasons," doubtless. No difficulty in assigning them. Only, if there has been one happening more than any other which has revealed to those outside the war atmosphere, the utter negation of personal life and moral law that is covered by our easy talk of " strategy," " tactics," and " moves," it has been this further persecution of the Belgian people. We may discuss it, as critics, as an excusable part of a defensive campaign. We feel in our hearts, that it is no other than the instinctive ferocity of the beast of prey, headed

294

off its next kill, and recoiling to savage its last victim.

War, the war of Ilium, of Agincourt, of Waterloo, used to be a brilliant affair. Death harnessed to a glittering car of Juggernaut. Men went under the wheels in the rush and flame of colours, and to the sound of bands and the applause of multitudes. The car is now hidden in a dull, deadly rolling cloud. We can only hear the rumour of the hidden wheels. Our sons and friends move into the darkness. Of many of them, all we shall ever know is that they have not returned. The greater heroes, that they go as gladly as ever did a chosen knight into crowded lists. The finer men, that they fight as stoutly with no record of their gallantry, no mark even of their death-place.

But we must make no confusion. It is the men who are to be praised: for their sacrifice of all they know to be better in life, for their acceptance of the fantastic chance which is forced upon them by their devotion to an ideal.

FROM THE TRENCHES

War itself, fighting, is a mad anachronism. We can judge of its folly the better, because we are now allowed to know so little of its secret noise and flame. We are not dazzled by its incidents; but its shadow falls on us all.

But then, afterwards, there must be no sentimentalising over the glitter of a splendour we have not seen; no wilful blindness when, the cloud cleared away, the light of sanity falls again upon the nakedness of its inhuman mechanism, the hideous squalor and vulgarity of its monstrous destructiveness.

A few days ago I was waiting with a crowd outside a Bureau in Paris. Anxious, resigned faces passed me going in or out. No tragedy, no moving emotion. The families of the soldiers in the front were making their weekly inquiry for the little numbered disc each soldier wears for identification. The best they could hope for was to receive nothing, to have to come and ask again, and again, till the end of the war. The only break would come when the little disc at last might be handed them, and they would know that son or husband, somewhere, somehow, had vanished in the shadow of war for all time.

In Wavre, where I used to pass continually on the way to the Belgian lines, was a small welcome restaurant, kept by a cheerful pretty girl, her young husband, and a baby. There was laugh and joke as to " what would happen if the Prussians came !" On the morning of the day of evacuation I passed again. Still only quiet anxiety and less ready smiles. Three hours later I returned. The Uhlans were entering the edges of the town. A peasant rushed into the swarming square, waving a Uhlan helmet. There was a savage rush ; and a woman shrieked : " It's the head of the devil who wore it I want !" It was the young wife. A fury, raging at her husband ; for the men had been told to disarm. "Take it," she screamed furiously, thrusting his rifle at him," never see me again, if our house is entered without one brute shot." Blanched, shaking with passion, and speechless, the young man walked out. I saw her again on the road to Brussels, aged, scarcely sane. The man had not come back. She had lost her child.

In west Flanders, on the day that the Prussian columns were pouring across Belgium, I passed in the morning a remote, picturesque little crossing. A very old peasant, in a smock, deaf and almost blind, acting as a Civil Guard, gave me great difficulty. He had blocked the road with harrows, and threatened viciously with an old muzzle-loader and rusty bayonet of the time of Waterloo. In the evening, carrying some wounded soldiers, we passed again. He was still hugging the bayonet. We persuaded him to let us bury it, his useless death-warrant, for the Uhlans were flooding behind us. With that, realisation at last came to him. He walked deliberately back towards the cottage. " All that I had left, for my son is dead. But I will destroy this too. The Prussians shall not shelter there."

The same night I was driving on the long

dark roads back to the coast. Occasionally the lights flashed on lines of women, in widows' black, returning in silence from the shrines. Now and again a blaze of light startled us from the roadside. The shrines of saints, bright with votive candles all this night of terror. And remote from their homesteads, and from the war, the heads of crowds of small children showed black on the steps against the altar lights; while in a semicircle on the road outside knelt the shadows of women, enclosing their children, the last possession left to them. I stopped the car before one shrine, and a high woman's voice, in which all emotion was dead, called out from the darkness: "Is that death?"

South of Peronne, hardly a week ago, we gave a lift to four refugee peasant-women, trudging heavily back to their homes. Two weeks before some German cavalry had swept suddenly into their small village. Ten men had been ordered to go with them, the husbands of two of the women, the sons of two others. They had disappeared in the shadow, and not one had returned. We reached the outlying cottage of the first. Some small skirmish had raged there. The house was half destroyed, and three or four dead horses lay grotesquely rotting on the field. The woman stood for a moment unmoved, and then turned to a neighbour : " War has taken my sons, and has left me these."

Four days ago a French soldier of the line stopped me just south of Vic-sur-Aisnes. He was hobbling back from the trenches, wounded in the knee. He was clearly half stupid with fatigue and the detonation of the days of firing. He kept repeating to himself, over and over again : " I cannot remember : there were five, all killed near me ; and three said to tell somebody a message, before they died. I cannot remember what it was, or who they were. I cannot remember : there were five——" and so over again. These were the last messages out of the edge of the shadow, and they were lost. But there would always be the discs. Better

that the details should not come. There would
then be still the chance of imagining some heroic
setting of death.

We may well remember that such death is
heroic, whatever its loneliness or its revolting
circumstances. But let us borrow no false
colour from an imaginary pomp and circum-
stance in war itself. It is dissolution and the
end of hope that is hidden in the cloud. In
England we are happily still free to interpret
the obscurity according to our fancy, to picture
death in battle as somehow not death. For
those who have moved by the edge of the shadow
there is no illusion left. The cloud shifts from
village to village, from week to week, only to let
us see in its track nature outraged, emotion
degraded, humanity defaced.

We have chosen war, and must follow it to
its undiscriminating end. Let us see to it that
it is for the last time.

CHAPTER XIV

Arms and the Man

There must be no misunderstanding. We may condemn the futility of the appeal to arms as the ultimate method of arbitriment between civilised beings; we can have nothing but whole-hearted admiration for the man who has answered the appeal.

Civilisation, if it means anything, has meant the development of the sense of humour. It was the gradual realisation of an absurd disconnection between seeing a man scowling, and clubbing the life out of him so that *he* should see no more, and between hearing his insults, and depriving *him* for all time of hearing, that brought primitive man out of savagery. The same discovery, of its incongruity put an end to the duel among us. Our German opponents have always been behind us in this, in civilisation, in the sense of humour. It is with a feeling of disgust as much as of anger that we find our civilisation cannot save us from being dragged down to the level of savage brawling.

But the appeal to arms once made, and our national and personal ideals once involved in the hazard, we may well be proud of the sane, temperate spirit with which the men of our race assert their superiority, even in the whirlpool of elemental passions that is war. Actual fighting, the killing of men, cannot be done well except by men in the rage of the fighting fever, in the passion that " sees red."—It is no surprise to us that the British soldier can still charge like seven demons. To lie for hours passive under fire, with death close round in the trenches, calls for a still rarer emotional concentration, the white animosity that flares steadily but does not flicker.—To those who know our history, it is no news that the Briton, for cold unshaken courage, can still out-last all other men.   But what, in a Briton, who has seen the soldiers of several nations reacting under the war-fever, touches a deeper chord of pride, is to see that our countrymen can pass in and out of the " fighting state " with the mental detachment of civilised beings.   Even in the " red rage " they become neither blind nor deaf to the call of humanity or reason.   They maintain personality against the overwhelming war atmosphere of animal fury and suspicion.   When the fighting shadow passes, they are still their natural selves, kindly or surly, or intelligent, knowing what they like or dislike, with no collective infection from a false pride, a simulated enthusiasm or hatred.

Of this power of maintaining mental balance, through all the flux and reflux of the " fighting state," military record gives us little idea. But it is the deciding factor in racial wars. The degree of its possession by the several races in the end decides for victory or failure. The nation that has the strongest vital stock survives longest. As between two such vital races in conflict, that must prevail which is the better " civilised "; which can maintain its characteristic strength, its individual consciousness, against all the assaults of violent physical or mental emotion.

A captured Prussian lieutenant, with whom I had a quick talk beside the road near Rheims a few days ago, was pleased to express surprise at the courage and doggedness of our British " mercenaries," as he called them. He thought I was insulting him, when I told him that the conditions under which our volunteer private served were very similar to those of the German officer !

It has been always a new surprise to find how many Germans, even those who know military history and are well acquainted with England, have allowed their sense of national rivalry with us, of jealousy rather than hatred, to blind their judgment, otherwise expert in military matters. They have continued to make three elementary blunders about our army; and they are now paying dearly for the miscalculation.

The first blunder has been to confuse a man who volunteers to fight for his own country, as his profession, with a " mercenary "; by which we mean a man who hires himself out to fight for any country which offers him enough pay. The second has been in some way to reason that a man who voluntarily makes himself efficient to defend his own country, and receives an allowance for it, must be inferior, as fighting material, to a man who compulsorily so serves his country, and receives an allowance for it. And the third has been the astounding ignorance of the teaching of military history, which proves conclusively that, from the time when the Spartans beat the Athenians down to the present day, the professional-soldier army has always beaten the amateur or conscript army, even at great disadvantage of numbers.

That is the essential difference which we have been seeing every day in the field. Our men

ARMS AND THE MAN

are fighting, just as consciously, for the preservation and honour of their country, as are their conscript enemies. But, because of their race, they do not care to make a parade of that consciousness. We do not encourage in war more than in peace the " jelly-bellied flag-flappers " whom Mr. Kipling has pilloried. It takes a very special story of pluck to draw from any collection of our soldiers even a " Good old England ! " or a " What will they say at home to that ? " Fighting, manœuvre, fatigue, firing, wounds, death, they are all just parts of their professional job ; which they like to do well for its own sake, and in which they have a technical interest.

When the fighting is done, in camp, in reserve, in intervals, it is striking to see the different look on the faces of the different races. The Briton keeps nothing of the fixed " war " look, the strained, set expression and eyes of some other races, as if the weight of a country was on their shoulders, as if death was near in thought and always being defied, as if the whole world was

307

an object of suspicion. The moment his "job" of fighting, or whatever it may be, is done for the time, the Briton becomes himself again. Just a tired and gay, or a tired and grumbly fellow who has finished his job, according to his ordinary nature.

England and his home and family have not been saved with every shot he has fired, and when he is off duty, he is not worried about the future of the Fatherland. He has learned in a hard school that his duty is just his job; and he has learned to do his job, killing, cooking, or horse-tending, with a keen, impersonal, professional interest.

When I said something like this to a German officer in prison at Bruges, he jumped at it: "Ah, just so! He fights like a machine: he has no heart in it! He will be beaten by our Germans, inspired by the one thought of the German flag!"

Not a bit! A boxer does not do less damage because he has learned how to fight, as an art,

with years of training. When he is in the ring,
heart tells in the end, but it tells through the
degree of skill. When you have got a soldier
who fights for the love of it, as a profession,
and, besides that, has become a master of
the art, you have found a champion who
will outlast a rank of compulsory-service
amateurs inspired by all the patriotism under
the sun!

Put our volunteer professionals in the firing
line, leave them to fend for themselves on a
terrible retreat, like that from Courtrai, and
the individual grit, the racial inspiration will
carry them through to the marvel of the world.
Their training will stand them in all the better
stead. They will know how to fight, what to
do, even when their company officers have fallen,
when they have lost their unit. Patriotism,
personality, they are there behind the professional keenness, as a driving, reserve force. Our
machine is not a barrel organ grinding out " Die
Wacht am Rhein," which wants the big handle

turned to keep the machinery going. Break the living organism, and each cell will remain instinct with life.

What strikes the Continental troops most is our soldiers' gaiety! It is not that the men are excitedly funny or tuneful, in trench or camp. (Our songs the French consider funereal!) But between fights they become just themselves again. The fighting job is over for the moment. It would be absurd among fellow professionals to make a fuss about it. The eternal grumbling Briton grumbles still, about his wet feet (he has just come in from fifteen hours under fire in the muddy trenches); about his food, traditional subject of caustic jest; about some old " puffing Sal," a howitzer that made a mark of his trench all day. He will talk of the mud she scattered over him, not probably of the pals hit on either side of him. Such grumbling seems to the Continental trooper a joke, a tremendous social effort. The cheery man rags as heartily as he ever would. The unsociable man sets to wash-

310

ing or eating imperturbably. What is there to make a fuss about ?

Of course, if an outsider like myself spoke at such times of the day's fighting, the men would lighten up with the interest of professionals, anxious to explain things. " We were on in that ball-room show "; " The—— and the —— caught it hot there "; " Nice little bit of shooting the Germans did there "; " Never knew we were hit and stood like sillies "; and then perhaps a stiff argument about the merits of " Ruddy Jim " or " Old Cough-drop," which would, as likely as not, prove to be two of the enemy's batteries that had been giving murderous trouble.

No wonder the foreign comrade, with his serious conception of the great danger and great issues that lay behind such affectionate nick-names, would listen astonished, and wonder how they "keep it up." Keep it up ? It is just themselves ! Unimaginative, humorous, businesslike men at their work, boys in their ways of thought and speech off duty.

FROM THE TRENCHES

The letters home are on the same reserved but natural note. Professional information being barred, the soldier has had to fall back on the few conventional phrases to express personal feelings, which our tongue-tied nation allows itself. They are learned in childhood, and so come easily.

It was often the same scene. In some deserted little village, dusty, sun-white, and shuttered, the glimpse of a khaki coat and a sun-red British face has cheered and checked us as we ran through.

Pleasant to hear the broad easy tongue; and we retire to the one little wine-shop, that still keeps open because it is near a base-camp.

The rumour of English newspapers in some unaccountable way gets abroad. Soon there are a dozen or more khaki caps crowded in the little room. The few peasants left drift in there too. The usual long handskakes, absurd French tags of talk. The soldiers are plundered of their last emblems, as mementoes. Not a village in the war area where one does not see peasant caps and peasant frocks decorated proudly with the insignia of some one of the British regiments.

Then comes talk of the chance of getting a letter home. Half of the men retire to violent wrestles with foreign pens and ink at the table in the rear of the shop: the rest stay yarning.

The letters are always read aloud or left open as a point of honour; but I had never once to suggest the omission of a line which gave place or date or regimental names. The tradition of the silent war has gone deep. Further, very few either knew or cared where they were or had been. The names meant nothing. Even the sense of time had been lost in the constant occupation and the turning of day into night.

Certainly the letters I saw at that end were far less picturesque than those published in the papers; but the latter, of course, are a selected number. The traditional " English tongue " learned in the elementary school, with its stiff conventions, held the paper. These scraps are typical of many read to me :   .

"Dear brother,—I hope you are well, as this leaves me. I am quite well. And I have not written before, as there has been no time. And I hope She and all are well. Please give them my love. I have seen ——, and we have seen lots of fighting. I think that is all, so must end. Love to —— and ——.—Yours affectionately, etc."

"Dear Dad,—This is the first time I have written, and I have had no letter. Please write soon, and ask Mum and sisters to write. I am quite well, as I hope this finds you. It is very hot, and it is bad for the horses. Baby Bob must be a big chap now. Give him my love. A gentleman is taking this. Tell all to write and send some cigarettes.

I will not write any more, so will end.—

From, etc.

ARMS AND THE MAN

Sometimes the human touch breaks through the conventions, in a kiss sent to a baby or in a scrawled P.S. :

"Dear Mother,—I am very well, as I hope you are and father. And —— and ——. It has been very hot, and I have not slept in bed for four weeks. But I am all serene. Give Tom my love, and I am glad he has joined; we must all do something. Don't worry.—From your loving son,——."

—and then a big scrawl all across the reverse sheet, and again the big scrawl across the back that brings a catch to one's throat—"Don't Worry, Mother." "DON'T WORRY."

I don't suppose they bothered much at home, when they got these letters, at the absence of battle news. Husband, brother, or son, the sight of his writing is enough. "I am quite well"—and for those waiting another milestone in their shadow-time has been safely passed.

315

FROM THE TRENCHES

In many of the Irish letters the mode is more picturesque, the expression comes easier.

" Dear——, —We got it last night but one, and J—— and C—— went home, God send they meet no Germans there. J—— had it in for them since big Tom went. I'm as I was, with a chip off my foot that's healing fine, and I hope you're doing well in these bad times. They have a story here that the German's firing silver bullets, as the leads run low. If I got a few in me, I'll bring them home to set you up. Send all the cigarettes you can find and chocolates. This is hell, and I have no time to write, the kisses is for yourself, but I expect the girls will steal them off the paper. Keep laughing, woman.—Your affekt. boy, ——."

This, again, is from a very young north Irishman :

" Dear Wife,—I have not written before,

for my time has been full up. If it's not all right about the money go to Mrs. ——. She has a good heart. Write soon, and send some cigarettes. How is little Dick ? Give him a kiss. He must be a great man now in this long while. Give my love to the old lady, and write soon, soon, SOON. I am wading in blood.—Your affectionate husband, ——."

He had not actually seen any fighting ; but the " neighbours " would want that battle touch for their talk, and so good manners demanded it.

Little scrawls, on scraps of paper, written on a stone or rifle-butt, they were shoved into my hands. Sometimes given by word of mouth.

" I hope you are quite well, as this leaves me," comes to have the force of a symbol, when we think of the remote homes to which the conventional phrase will mean so much. In fancy

FROM THE TRENCHES

we can follow each of them, by sea, and rail, and cart, to the moment of the postman's knock, the opening door. . . .

Wyman & Sons Ltd., Printers, London and Reading.

Lightning Source UK Ltd.
Milton Keynes UK
UKOW05f1256210915

259000UK00014B/627/P